D0205371

THE QUESTION OF REALITY

THE QUESTION OF REALITY

o o o

Milton K. Munitz

Princeton University Press
Princeton, New Jersey

Library of Congress Cataloging-in-Publication Data
Munitz, Milton Karl, 1913-
The question of reality / Milton K. Munitz.
p.   cm.
Includes index.
ISBN 0-691-07362-7 (alk. paper)
1. Reality. 2. Creation. 3. Truth. 4. Knowledge, Theory of.
I. Title.
BD331.M87 1990
111—dc20   89-10210   CIP

Publication of this book has been aided by
the Whitney Darrow Publication Reserve Fund
of Princeton University Press

This book has been composed in Linotron Electra with Weiss

Princeton University Press books are printed
on acid-free paper, and meet the guidelines
for permanence and durability of the
Committee on Production Guidelines
for Book Longevity of the
Council on Library Resources

Printed in the United States of America
by Princeton University Press,
Princeton, New Jersey

10 9 8 7 6 5 4 3 2 1

Contents

v

Preface

Despite recurrent efforts to call into question the prospects—indeed the very meaningfulness—of adequately satisfying the human drive to achieve a correct picture of the nature of reality on its most comprehensive scale, the pursuit of this goal shows no signs of abatement. In our own day, as in earlier epochs, we have witnessed major onslaughts on the soundness of such metaphysical ambitions, and in our own day, too, we have seen how many have found, at least to their own satisfaction, ways of deflecting and overcoming these attacks.

In these discussions, there is, to be sure, no consensus on the scope of metaphysics or its methods. Yet even the most cynical and skeptical of critics has to acknowledge on purely historical, psychological, or cultural grounds the existence of an abiding matrix of metaphysical motivations associated with the need felt by those who want to meet the challenge of our common human situation by coming to terms, intellectually and spiritually, with the world in which we live.

Overlaying and punctuating these abiding incentives are certain questions that come into prominence at particular stages of history and that serve as special entry points to the wider field of metaphysics. Frequently these questions are provoked by crises of a religious or scientific sort. Answering these questions involves giving consideration to such fundamental matters as how to conceive of the nature of truth, the scope of human knowledge, and the fundamental dimensions of reality. These intellectual crises accordingly call forth the deepest and most far-flung exertions of the human mind: they belong to metaphysics.

Take, for example, recent revolutionary scientific discoveries in cosmology and particle physics. When we read that scientists have come close to pinpointing the "origin of the universe" by means of a Big Bang cosmology, or are engaged in formulating a "theory of everything," as in current ten-dimensional superstring theories of particle physics, can we doubt that such inquiries or their results, when examined, inevitably raise questions of a metaphysical and epistemological sort, and that in order to respond to them it is no longer acceptable to avoid or dismiss, in wholesale fashion, such philosophical topics on the ground that they are futile, meaningless, or irresolvable? Like it or not, we must once again join the fray, examine the options, justify our opinions, and take sides.

This book is a companion volume to my recently published *Cosmic Understanding.*[1] It can be read independently of the latter and its argument is self-contained. In the earlier book, I was primarily concerned with exploring what is involved in the use by recent cosmology of the notions of the "beginning" and "end" of the universe. "How," I asked, "are these temporally oriented concepts of 'beginning' and 'end' to be understood when applied to the universe as compared to their use in connection with various entities *in* the universe—for example, the birth and death of an organism or a star?" In offering my answer to this question, I argued for the superior merit of regarding the use of the terms "beginning" and "end," when applied to the universe, not as marking objective *events* in the history of a comprehensive physical object (what many believe the universe to be), but, instead, as *conceptual horizons* that arise from the use of certain special

---

[1] Milton K. Munitz, *Cosmic Understanding: Philosophy and Science of the Universe* (Princeton, N.J.: Princeton University Press, 1986).

theories and models of cosmological scope that have been created by human beings.

In this volume, I take as my principal theme two interrelated matters. One is the major intellectual dominance in the history of Western thought of the notion of cosmic creation, together with the associated view that truth, when found, consists in the *disclosure* of the inherent intelligible structure imposed on the world at its creation. The impact of this conception of truth as "disclosure" persists throughout many variations of the philosophy of epistemological realism, though it is often disengaged from a theistic metaphysics and its doctrine of cosmic creation. A second theme centers on the consequences for our view of reality and truth that would flow from taking a broadly "Kantian" approach, as exemplified especially in the later writings of Ludwig Wittgenstein. For such an orientation, stress is placed on the autonomous and creative role played by scientific schemes of thought and by languages of various sorts, brought into operation by human beings for the purpose of making our experience of the world intelligible.

By taking this latter Kantian reorientation as my own preferred point of departure, we must re-examine what we mean by "truth" and "intelligible order." In attempting to meet this need, and in contrast to what is involved with appraising certain human beliefs as "true" and as offering legitimate instances of knowledge, I argue at the same time for recognizing a level of radical *unintelligibility* in reality that defeats all hopes of its being amenable to understanding and knowledge. I use the expression "Boundless Existence" for this purpose, and undertake to show how we are led to an awareness of this dimension of reality through a number of considerations of a cosmological and epistemological character. In distinction from the traditional view that assigns to a Cosmic Creator the role of bringing the world into existence and endowing it with an objective, discoverable, inherent structure, the "Kantian" approach (as here employed) gives special attention to the *human* contributions to making the universe intelligible, while it also obliges us to resign ourselves to leaving the very existence of the universe unaccounted for.

In brief, I will approach the treatment of the question of reality—and whether or to what extent it can be "answered"—on two levels. I will argue that on one level, *there is* an answer to the question of reality, insofar as (1) one discriminates two major dimensions of reality, *viz.*, the observable universe and Boundless Existence; and (2) by means of humanly devised conceptual schemes, one renders intelligible the various properties, contents, and structures of the observable universe. On another level, however, the question of reality *is not answerable* at all—and this is due to the utter unintelligibility of Boundless Existence as a fundamental aspect of reality. This unintelligibility of Boundless Existence is in no way lessened or removed, however far science has already progressed or may continue to advance in achieving intelligibility with respect to the contents, scope, evolutionary development, and internal structures of the universe.

The material to be covered is divided into two principal parts. In Part One, "Inherited Guidelines," I review some relevant features of the thought of Plato, Kant, and Wittgenstein—material with which some readers may already have familiarity. These ideas serve as an important backdrop and preparation for Part Two, "Between An Answer and No Answer," where I offer my own suggestions about how to respond to "the central question of reality."

Chapter 5 contains material on which I based a paper entitled "The Scope of Cosmic Understanding," presented at a conference on "The Origin of the Universe" held at Colorado State University, September 1988.

I wish to thank Sanford G. Thatcher and Alice Calaprice, editors at Princeton University Press, for their valuable suggestions in the editing of my manuscript.

Scarborough, New York
April 1989

THE QUESTION OF REALITY

Central Questions

Many philosophers, religiously oriented individuals, and thoughtful, reflective persons have given varied expression to what, for them, constitutes "the central question" or "the matter of ultimate concern." The question is regarded as *central* and the concern *ultimate*, inasmuch as any answers would be expected to yield an all-encompassing framework of basic beliefs, underlying commitments, and associated attitudes toward life that would have the widest-ranging kind of influence in dealing with questions of narrower scope or of more restricted concern, whatever the degree of intensity and urgency of the latter.

The following are some familiar examples of this type of question or concern: What is the meaning of life? What is the ultimate ground of human existence? What is the nature and origin of the Universe? Why is there Something rather than Nothing? Does the existence of the Universe have a purpose, and does its structure exhibit a grand design? Is there a God? What are the fundamental forms, domains, modes, and dimensions of reality? Is there an absolute, objective truth about reality which, if known, would render it wholly intelligible?

That one can formulate the central question or matter of ultimate concern in various ways shows that there is no well-established consensus about how this is to be done. There are of course many points of overlap among these formulations, since it would be found that any reasonably full reply to any one of them also involves treating many of the topics considered in the others. Not one of these central questions or statements of ultimate concern exists in a self-contained, isolated compartment of its own. It is nevertheless true that each formulation displays a special preference for what, in the view of one who shows this preference, calls for *primary* attention.

The question that looks for an answer to the meaning of life (or, as it is also sometimes phrased, "the ultimate ground of human existence") takes its point of departure from a sensitivity to and preoccupation with the opportunities, crises, and limitations of the human situation. Sometimes the raising of this form of question arises in acutely experienced periods of crisis in the life of an entire group or of an individual person—for example, in facing the fact of death or in a pervasive and enduring collapse of an overall sense of purpose and direction in one's life. For the individual, at such moments or during such periods, the psyche cries out for help, and the person desperately seeks for an answer to overcome the void and an enervating sense of despair. In the face of such extreme situations, there is a deeply felt need about how to make sense of life, how to justify its continuation. What is looked for is some convincing answer that would restore a meaningful direction to life, an answer that would supply some form of hope, or (failing that) at least provide a genuinely felt attitude of resignation in the face of "the inevitable."

The raising of this kind of question, however, is not confined to moments of crisis. It emerges and demands an answer even in moments of relative peace and well-being. We may ask ourselves the following: Why are we here at all? How shall we look at our existence as human beings? What does it all amount to? Shouldn't we say, perhaps, that any achievement—minor or major, personal or collective—is bound to be swallowed up sooner or later in total oblivion and thereby made to count for nought in some final reckoning of pluses and minuses? These kinds of questions look for some satisfying answer, an answer that we can have confidence in, that leaves us in peace and does not constantly reawaken the fundamental human craving to which it responds. The answer is believed to be of overriding importance beyond any others that an individual may find; when asked on a broader canvas in behalf of a larger group or even mankind at large, it is the most far-reaching in its general impact. Questions such as these come to light when we look for fundamental guidance, both in the present and into the foreseeable future, in understanding our human situation.

What we seek is a philosophy of life. Although at various points this need overlaps some of the questions the discipline of Ethics raises (where "Ethics" is understood as an inquiry into what is right or wrong), a philosophy of life goes beyond ethical questions in this more restricted sense. Instead, it looks at life in its total setting. It looks to beginnings and endings, to opportunities and goals, to given conditions and to ideal goods—in short, to what justifies human existence when seen on the broadest scale. It looks for some way of accomplishing a comprehensive reckoning that would help determine whether, or to what extent, life is worth living at all. How should such a philosophy of life be given adequate formulation?

Another type of central question is variously phrased as follows: Is there a God? Does God exist? Should I believe in God? Other, more specific yet related ways of asking this type of question are: How shall we understand the first sentence of the Book of Genesis in the Bible: "In the beginning God created the heaven and the earth"? Should we accept this statement as conveying a centrally important truth in our conception of the nature of reality? Not only are there many different interpretations of the *meaning* of this opening sentence of the Bible, but also varied and conflicting judgments with respect to its *truth-value*. The replies to these questions include evaluative judgments that range over a wide spectrum, among which are those that regard the sentence as meaningful and true; others that regard it as undecidable, meaningless, false; or still others that give it no serious interest at all.

A closely related way of posing this type of central question is to elicit a response to Nietzsche's famous pronouncement: "God is dead!" One well-known passage in which Nietzsche makes this dramatic claim is the following:

> Have you not heard of that madman who lit a lantern in the bright morning hours, ran to the market place, and cried incessantly, "I seek God! I seek God!" As many of those who do not believe in God were standing around just then, he provoked much laughter. Why, did he get lost? said one. Did he lose his way like a child? said another. Or is he hiding? Is he afraid of us? Has he gone on a voyage? or emigrated? Thus they yelled and laughed. The madman jumped into their midst and pierced them with his glances.
>
> "Whither is God?" he cried. "I shall tell you. We *have killed him*—you and I. All of us are his murderers. But how have we done this? How were we able to drink up the sea? Who gave us the sponge to wipe away the entire horizon? What did we do when we unchained this earth from its sun? Whither is it moving now? Whither are we moving now? Away from all suns? Are we not plunging continually? Backward, sideward, forward, in all directions? Is there any up or down left? Are we not straying as through an infinite nothing? Do we not feel the breath of empty space? Has it not become colder? Is not night and more night coming on all the while? . . . God is dead. God remains dead. And we have killed him. . . . What was holiest and most powerful of all that the world has yet owned has bled to death under our knives. Who will wipe this blood off us? . . ."
>
> Here the madman fell silent and looked again at his listeners; and they too were silent and stared at him in astonishment. At last he threw his lantern on the ground, and it broke and went out. "I come too early," he said then; "my time has not come yet. This tremendous event is still on its way . . .—it has not yet reached the ears of man. Lightning and thunder require time, the light of the stars requires time, deeds require time even after they are done, before they can be seen and heard. This deed is still more distant

from them than the most distant stars—*and yet they have done it themselves.*"

It has been related further that on that same day the madman entered divers churches and there sang his *requiem aeternam deo.*[1]

How shall we judge Nietzsche's pronouncement and the challenge it poses? Does it tell us something both true and important about our present intellectual, spiritual, and cultural situation? Does it mark a crisis in human development? If so, how can it be met?

Let us now, finally, consider a type of central question asked by many—one that looks for ways of formulating an acceptable general theory of the nature of being, reality, existence, the world at large. This is the concern of metaphysics, ontology, or (as some prefer to say) a world view.

To forestall any misunderstanding, let me remark that my use of the expression "world at large" should be differentiated from other common uses of the term "world." Thus in popular usage the term "world" is sometimes employed in a broadly astronomical orientation to describe, for example, our planet Earth or some other planet in the solar system; a star or galaxy; or the universe in its most general features and contents as investigated by the astronomer and cosmologist. Another common role for "world" is to serve as a designation for the inclusive domain of human affairs or some special subdivision of it (e.g., the business world or the art world), especially contemporaneous ones, in distinction from the activities and involvements of a personal or private sort; and still another as a designation for a special domain of interest, say a hobby or preoccupation that one or more persons may have—for example, the world of stamp-collecting. In addition, there are also certain special uses of the term "world" in philosophy that should be distinguished from the present use

---

[1] Friedrich Nietzsche, *Die Fröhliche Wissenschaft* (The Gay Science), 125. Translation by Walter Kaufmann, in his *Nietzsche* (Princeton, N.J.: Princeton University Press, 1950), chap. 3.

of the expression "world at large." Thus, for a Platonist, there is a fundamental distinction between "the intelligible world of Forms" and "the world of material, sensible entities." Again, for the Cartesian-inspired tradition of epistemology in modern philosophy, a typical contrast is drawn between "the inner world of mental phenomena" and the "external, physical world." Finally, there is the traditional theist's distinction between "the world created by God" and "the transcendent, other-worldly being of God." All these special uses of "world" are examples, at best, *within* the broadly conceived interest in the world at large, where the latter is the target of a *world view, metaphysics,* or *ontology.*

The use of the expression "world view" exemplifies a type of preference increasingly found not only in everyday speech but in the discourse of many philosophers and scientists. Unlike the use of the term "metaphysics," especially—which for many persons suggests inquiries into matters that lie beyond Nature or the sphere of what is open to observational experience, and therefore is to be eschewed—the expression "world view" is accordingly preferred because it is thought to be less pejorative, less encumbered by unwanted associations that cling to the expression "metaphysics." My own use of the expressions "metaphysics," "ontology," and "world view" makes them interchangeable when my purpose is, as indeed it is at the moment, to direct attention preanalytically to the widest possible subject matter about whose nature, structure, dimensions, or properties we seek to acquire a set of defensible beliefs—or even those for which we can reach no creditable knowledge at all.

It is widely acknowledged, even by those who despair of reaching satisfactory answers to this type of question, that there is an irrepressible need and persistent hunger on the part of human beings—in all periods of history, in all cultures, and equipped with the most diverse degrees of intellectual sophistication and varied methods of approach—to try to answer it. It voices a need to have some overall picture, view, conception, system, theory, or call it what you will, of how to characterize the most fundamental dimensions, modes, and levels of reality, being, existence, the world at large.

From the days of classical Greek philosophy to the present, many have looked to metaphysics to examine critically various ways of responding to this question. In the view of those who give primary place to this way of phrasing the central question, the interest of metaphysics plays a foundational role with respect to all other disciplines, lines of inquiry, and types of intellectual interest. To have a considered view concerning the nature of reality provides the most inclusive and overarching framework for such philosophic disciplines as logic, ethics, and epistemology, as well as for what is encompassed under such fields as mathematics, science, art, politics, law, history, and religion. Indeed, it is commonly believed that questions concerning the nature of reality are those to which all the other central questions previously posed—for all their importance and genuine interest—are themselves only so many different routes.

When we examine the results of the many-sided efforts devoted to this topic, both in their earlier and contemporary examples, we find that widespread differences exist among them. Such differences are in some cases linked to the names of prominent philosophers—for example, "Platonist," "Aristotelian," "Thomist," "Cartesian," "Spinozist," "Leibnizian," "Hegelian," "Heideggerian," "Whiteheadian," etc.—while others receive classificatory "ism" labels, for example, "theism," "naturalism," "idealism," and so on.

Furthermore, not all theories of reality receive the same degree of articulation and care of expression: some are relatively crude, others highly sophisticated and complicated. Again, while some are relatively static and unchanging over long periods of time, others show greater flexibility and receptivity to change. There are, finally, important and noticeable differences that reflect the manifold contributions from different cultural sources (mythology, the arts, social ideologies, religion, and science), which thereby account for their distinctive emphases and orientation.

In the light of all this, the makeup of a particular theory of reality—the content and organization of its ideas and beliefs with respect to the entities or dimensions it recognizes and the modes of knowing them—will vary as we go from one to another. In addition to these noticeable differences, there are also, of course, overlapping or close similarities among them. In short, there is no single or final way of plotting the conceptual geography, history, or taxonomy of theories of reality. And for the philosopher or historian of thought interested in this area of investigation, it is an endless though fascinating task to find better and more rewarding ways of charting the differences, similarities, sources, influences, and diverse types of cultural impact associated with these various metaphysical theories.

History, accordingly, reveals not only a wide range of proposals of how the basic human need for a metaphysical view is to be satisfied. It also offers an apparently endless series of controversies that arise from the claims of each contender to possess genuine knowledge afforded by his own metaphysical scheme in contrast to the truth-claims of other views, which he consequently rejects as false. The controversies thus engendered seem not only to proliferate but to be irresolvable. The contrast with the acknowledged progress to be found in other areas, such as in the sciences, arouses repeated attempts not only to account for this difference, but it also encourages various moves and programs that cast doubt upon the genuineness of the search for the kind of knowledge sought for, and would therefore call into question the entire effort to satisfy the metaphysical hunger. Thus, over the centuries, various challenges have been leveled against this type of search—voices of skepticism and derision toward those who persist in this allegedly quixotic, futile search.

A major example in recent thought of the drive to eliminate metaphysics as a legitimate branch of philosophic inquiry was the work of philosophers originally associated with the Vienna Circle, whose thought broadened into the philosophic movement known as Logical Positivism. Its greatest prominence and influence belonged to the period of the two world wars of the twentieth century.[2] Among positivists, one matter had unanimous agreement and defined one of the principal objectives of their movement: the elimination of metaphysics.[3] This goal was pursued on the grounds that the purported results of metaphysical inquiry are inherently *meaningless*. A principal basis for upholding this claim was adherence to the *principle of verifiability*. The adoption of this principle as a guide for *all* cognitive pursuits was modeled on its use in empirical science. Any meaningful statement in empirical science, it was maintained, satisfies the principle of verifiability: in advance of actual verificatory observations or experiments, one is required to specify the possible conditions for determining whether the statement could be supported by empirically obtained evidence. A meaningful statement is in principle *verifiable*, even though it may not yet have been actually *verified*. Consequently, if one encounters a purported meaningful statement that does not satisfy this criterion, it must be set down as in principle unverifiable, hence meaningless. And this, positivists agreed, is chronically the case with metaphysical statements. Whatever poetical, rhetorical, emotional, or edifying values metaphysical statements may admittedly possess, they have no genuine cognitive value. They are empirically unverifiable, hence not even true *or* false.

After much critical examination (even by those initially sympathetic to this view), it was generally recognized that the efforts to eliminate metaphysics totally by the proposed means were largely unsuccessful. One of the main weaknesses in these efforts concerned the logical status of the statement formulating the

[2] Cf. P. Achinstein and S. Barker, eds., *The Legacy of Logical Positivism for the Philosophy of Science* (Baltimore: The Johns Hopkins University Press, 1969); A. J. Ayer, *Language, Truth, and Logic*, 2d ed. (London: Victor Gollancz Ltd., and New York, Dover Publications, 1936); A. J. Ayer, ed., *Logical Positivism* (New York: Macmillan Publishing Co., 1959); Milton K. Munitz, *Contemporary Analytic Philosophy* (New York: Macmillan Publishing Co., 1981), 237–268.

[3] See Rudolf Carnap, "Überwindung der Metaphysik durch Logische Analyse der Sprache," *Erkenntnis*, vol. 2 (1932), trans. as "The Elimination of Metaphysics through Logical Analysis of Language," in Ayer, *Logical Positivism*, 60–81; Ayer, *Language, Truth, and Logic*, chap. 1.

principle of verifiability itself. The adoption of the principle could be regarded as offering part of what we mean by the use of the term "science." But this stipulative definition of "science" is a recommendation, a proposal for adopting a certain convention with respect to the use of this term. Even if it is accepted, this recommendation need not be binding with respect to determining the meaningfulness of metaphysical inquiries or judging the possible cognitive value of metaphysical statements. On the other hand, if the statement of the principle of verifiability is classified as an empirical hypothesis, hence open to disconfirmation by observational experience, it is possibly false. In either case, the appeal to the principle of verifiability would not be genuinely damaging or powerful enough to bring about the elimination of metaphysics. From these and other criticisms, it eventually became clear that the attempted elimination of metaphysics could not be accomplished by the means proposed.

Indeed, even the attempt to take seriously the recommendations of the positivists to turn to the pursuit of science for the genuine satisfaction of intellectual needs raises, afresh and insistently, a variety of questions that shows remarkable affinity and scope to those previously exorcised and condemned as unworthy of serious attention. For if we look into the course of inquiry in some of the central disciplines of twentieth-century science—for example, cosmology and quantum mechanics—we find that some basic questions of a metaphysical sort (now perhaps relabeled under the neutral-sounding heading of "world view") are encountered at the very frontiers of these inquiries as well.

With respect to the questions collected under the heading of "quantum reality," the famous debates between Einstein and Niels Bohr are a widely recognized example of this type of discussion. Some of the questions were the following: Do quantum systems possess properties only when they are measured or observed? Can different parts of a quantum system, widely separated in space, influence each other despite the absence of any known mechanism of interaction? Does science, at the level of the quantum, have to surrender adherence to the principle of causality?

Are individual quantum events completely describable in principle, or is there an inherent probabilistic element "in reality" that confines knowledge only to the description and explanation of ensembles of events?[4]

Moreover, beyond the specific problems of quantum reality, what is one to make of the status of theoretical concepts, generally, in science? What "contact," if any, do the theories of science make with reality? Further, if one surveys the history of scientific inquiry on its theoretical level, does this add up to a convergence on "the final truth"—a disclosure of what reality in fact is—or is the history of theories of science merely an interminable succession of incommensurable accounts in which each account needs to be judged only pragmatically and within a limited framework provided by a particular research program?

Among examples of the kinds of thought that prompt metaphysical inquiries and speculations, a major role is played by topics considered in cosmology. The interest in having a grasp of the fundamental structure and composition of the physical and astronomic universe has been a persistent one to which, over the centuries, various resources and cultural institutions have made their contribution.

Answers have been given by borrowing from the results of accumulated astronomic observations and appealing to the conceptual constructions of myth, religion, philosophy, and science. Even where the conception of the universe is quite primitive and consists in having a composite image of the observed patterns of locations and motions in the starlit sky, the rising and setting of the sun, the change of seasons, the phases of the moon, the earth

---

4 See Alastair Rae, *Quantum Physics: Illusion or Reality?* (Cambridge, Eng.: Cambridge University Press, 1986); Nick Herbert, *Quantum Reality* (Anchor Press, Doubleday, 1985); Euan Squires, *The Mystery of the Quantum World* (Boston and Bristol: Adam Hilger, 1986); Arthur Fine, *The Shaky Game: Einstein, Realism, and the Quantum Theory* (Chicago: University of Chicago Press, 1986); H. Krips, *The Metaphysics of Quantum Theory* (Oxford: Clarendon Press, 1987); M. Redhead, *Incompleteness, Non-Locality, and Realism* (Oxford: Oxford University Press, 1987).

beneath one's feet, the cycle of birth and death of animals and fellow human beings, questions of a familiar and recurrent sort inevitably arose in trying to make sense of this complex, changing, and encompassing panorama. Where did all this come from? Does it have a beginning? Will it have an end? What are the forces that control it? Is there a purpose behind it all? The questions themselves have received various formulations. In emerging from the first stirrings of vague, unfocused puzzlements, they have passed into questions that were expressed with increasingly greater sophistication, clarity, precision, and under the urgency of special presuppositional demands. Hints of such questions undoubtedly occurred to primitive man in the long, dark, prehistory of early human cultures. They were the seedbed for raising the kinds of questions that in time led to the fashioning of various myths and religious schemes of thought, whether animistic, polytheistic, or monotheistic. They were the kinds of questions, too (along with many other questions with which they were intertwined), that much later prompted the bold, imaginative, and shrewd speculations of the first philosophers and proto-scientists of our own Western tradition: the pre-Socratic Greek *physikoi* and cosmologists of sixth and fifth centuries B.C. An interest in cosmology and its ramifications has never died out, although one finds periods in its history and in its presence in different cultures that are marked by either relative stagnancy or active growth and change.

Today, questions of cosmological scope are once again pursued with revivified eagerness and energy, and with the aid of the most sophisticated tools of science. They are once more in the forefront of technical and widespread public interest as a result of important observational discoveries and novel physical theories. Recent investigations have led to the broad consensus that the universe began with a Big Bang approximately fifteen billion years ago, that it has already undergone various stages of physical and astronomical evolution and will undergo still other changes, and that it will eventually come to an end in the remote future.

An appreciation of the nature and scope of cosmology in the light of these recent scientific advances calls not only for a reasonably clear grasp of the fruits of research of the community of working cosmologists, but also, on another level, for a critical examination of a number of philosophical questions. Admittedly, these questions are normally eschewed by many cosmologists; or, if considered by some, they are given only secondary and occasional attention, since their energies and primary interests as scientists are normally devoted to carrying forward their daily data-gathering or theory-construction projects. Yet these broader philosophical questions will not go away. They take on a major importance for all those interested in assessing the wider significance of the goals and accomplishments of cosmology as a science.

The philosophical questions include the following: In what different senses can the term "universe" be used, and how are they related to one another? What are the different kinds of limits or horizons that the pursuit of cosmology confronts in the drive to understand the universe as a whole? Indeed, what do we mean when we use the concept "whole" in connection with the universe? If there are different senses of this concept, what advantages are there in the choice and application of one or another of these meanings? What does it mean to speak of the "beginning" or "end" of the universe? Can we apply these concepts to the universe in the same way in which they are used in connection with entities *within* the universe? When the cosmologist uses the conceptual resources of mathematical physics and the language of mathematics to construct cosmological models, are we to think of the use of these tools as means for uncovering the inherent, objective properties of the universe—properties having their own independent existence prior to human investigation—or is the adoption at a particular stage of inquiry of a cosmological model at best only the application of a human construct, whose value is to be determined pragmatically and not by any test of correspondence with putatively objective facts? Is the achievement of cosmic intelligibility the result of *conferring* intelligibility on observational data or of *discovering* it in some already existing entity? What bearing do recent cosmological theories of the beginning and end of the universe have on man's search for the meaning of life?[5]

In addition to the foregoing, a typical and recurrent cluster of metaphysical questions is the following: Is the universe, to the extent that it can be understood and known, all there is to reality? Insofar as cosmology succeeds increasingly in achieving some satisfactory account of the universe, is this success tantamount to making progress in understanding the fundamental nature of reality? Some would say "yes" to both questions. For them, the only "beyond" the universe is an even more satisfactory account than what is already known and understood, at any given stage of scientific inquiry, of the universe; and this deeper understanding and knowledge can be achieved only through the ongoing pursuit of scientific cosmology.

Others would demur at this reply. They look for another type of answer to the question of whether there is anything "beyond" the physical-universe-as-known that needs to be taken into account in adopting a satisfactory general theory of reality. Thus, traditional theism answers the foregoing questions in the affirmative: "beyond" the world (or universe) is God. God is the transcendent Creator of the universe and the ultimate source of cosmic existence, structure, and purpose.

Yet there is another way of incorporating a notion of transcendence in metaphysics, another conception of what exists "beyond" the universe. The possibility of giving such an alternative affirmative answer along lines wholly different from those offered by traditional theism will occupy us in the explorations that follow. I shall undertake to defend a world view that incorporates its own form of awareness of a transcendent dimension of reality: it uses the expression "Boundless Existence" for this purpose. Boundless Existence is "boundless" because it altogether eludes any form of conceptual boundedness or description—or the use of *any general conceptual terms whatsoever*. This approach to

[5] For a detailed discussion of these themes, see my book *Cosmic Understanding*.

metaphysical transcendence accordingly rejects not only the possibility of any success that attends efforts to remove the mystery of existence by resorting to a theological doctrine of creation; it also rejects reliance on the supposedly all-sufficing competence of science, which—it may be thought—if pursued long enough, should achieve "the final and total truth" about the nature of reality.

In supporting these claims, I shall focus attention on two central topics. One has to do with the use of the term "exists" (or its nominalization, "existence"). The other has to do with the term "intelligibility" and the extent to which what it stands for may be said to be manifested—or not—in human efforts to comprehend reality.

In connection with "existence," I shall concentrate my analysis on two major strands in its use. One of these is its role in referring to various particular *existents*; in particular, I shall focus on ways of analyzing the commonly held belief that the *universe* exists, is an *existent* of a special, comprehensive sort. The other is not concerned with particular existents, whatever their magnitude, complexity, evolutionary status, properties, or scope. This use is conveyed by the expression "Boundless Existence." I will use it to designate an aspect of reality that is not itself an existent or even the domain of existents taken collectively, yet is "present in" every existent.

As to the question of "intelligibility," I shall compare two main strands and traditions by which this concept has been interpreted. The dominant one, to be classified as *Platonic* and *realistic,* is linked with the notion of cosmic creation and supports the general belief that insofar as reality is intelligible, it rests upon the extent to which some putatively objective set of inherent properties or structural patterns can be *discovered* as belonging to the various types of *existents* that compose reality. The other way of interpreting "intelligibility" stresses the role human beings play in *constructing* and inventing various linguistic and conceptual schemes for rendering the materials of experience intelligible. Their deployment and application result in *conferring* intelligibility upon what we find in our encounters with the world. I shall label this approach to intelligibility the *Kantian* way of interpreting this concept, and I will show how in our own day Ludwig Wittgenstein (especially in his later writings) gave voice to this type of approach, though in highly modified form compared to the details of Kant's account.

My own pursuit of these themes will argue for the general thesis that the domain of existents (including the effort by science on its most comprehensive scale of interest to render the universe, as an existent, intelligible) can yield, at best, to the achievement of intelligibility only by Kantian means. By contrast, the transcendent status of Boundless Existence defeats all human efforts at making it intelligible, including the use of Kantian methods. It is the acceptance of this latter conclusion concerning the unintelligibility of Boundless Existence that is meant by the claim there is "no answer" to the question of reality.

The philosophic ideas to be reviewed in the next three chapters will be primarily of a historical character. As linked, respectively, to the philosophic views of Plato, Kant, and Wittgenstein, I shall consider three principal themes: (1) the traditional nexus of philosophic concepts of *cosmic creation*; *intelligibility* as an inherent, built-in feature of the structure of the cosmos; and *knowledge* as consisting in examples of human success in disclosing that structure (*realism*); (2) the turn, in modern philosophy, to a metaphysical and epistemological distinction between *appearance and reality*, exemplified in Kant's revolutionary philosophy of transcendental idealism, with its insistence on recognizing a fixed, a priori, necessary structure belonging to the ordering patterns and principles that the mind uses in the interpretation of the data of sensory experience; (3) Wittgenstein's treatment of *language* and his conception of *world pictures*: themes that carry forward the Kantian revolution, while in other ways sharply diverging from Kant's own views. The theme summarized in (1) will be examined in chapter 1, while the ideas referred to in (2) and (3) will be discussed in chapters 2 and 3.

My general purpose in offering this survey is to provide the background of ideas, distinctions, and critical judgments that will be appealed to in undertaking, in Part Two, the principal constructive goal of the present investigation: to formulate in what the question of reality consists, and to give grounds for determining, in broad outline, to what extent the question can or cannot be answered.

Part 1

∘ ∘ ∘

INHERITED
GUIDELINES

ONE

Cosmic Creation

COSMOGONIC MYTHS

It is impossible to draw a sharp line of division between the stage of human history in which cosmogonic myths are prevalent and the stage in which efforts at rational philosophic or proto-scientific inquiry emerged, as in sixth- and fifth-century B.C. Greece. Even if one does draw distinctions between prevalent modes of thought at different stages of human development or in different cultures, so that, for example, one can contrast "myth" and "science," the influence of myth lingers at least at the points of transition, and in a broad sense, moreover, never disappears altogether, since the reliance on analogy and metaphor to probe fresh or difficult areas of inquiry is present even on the level of the most sophisticated, advanced examples of human thinking.

Mankind's richly stored fund of cosmogonic myths gives clear evidence that there is hardly a source of analogy with some feature of familiar human experience that has not been put to imaginative and speculative use in accounting for the origin of the world: the world emerged as a small hill from the depths of the surrounding primeval waters; the world was born from a cosmic egg; the different regions of the world came into existence through the agency of a supremely powerful ruler who slew a dragon (or some other creature), cut up its carcass into major segments, and assigned them to subordinate gods; the world came into existence at the authoritative command of an all-powerful God. And so on.[1]

Aside from the cosmogonies preserved, for example, in Mesopotamian and Egyptian mythology that made use of particular features of local topography and geography in their generalizations about the conditions that prepared the ground for the origin of the world as a whole, other major sources of analogy for purposes of cosmogonic model building have been largely three in number: biological facts of birth and growth; modes of establishing social order; and the making of artifacts by skilled craftsmen.

If, from among the variety of mythic cosmogonies, one identifies certain models as being "obviously primitive," while others continue to win an underlying sympathetic resonance and understanding even though they are not accompanied by any commitment to their literal truth, this distinction finds its typical justification in various ways. It is there, for example, in the contrast made between an analogy drawn from thoughtful craftsmanship, on the one hand, and an analogy that, on the other hand, appeals to the mechanisms of biological generation, to geographical, meteorological, and physical facts, or, finally, to the manifold types of power, rule, and authority associated with different forms of communal or political life. For in the case of analogies drawn from geographical, physical, biological, or even social phenomena, one may assume the operation of causative conditions to be blind—lacking guidance by a deliberate plan. This naturally invites questions about the underlying conditions that could explain *their* coming into existence and operation.

In contrast, the situation is different in using the analogy of craftsmanship, at least with examples of recognized originality and creativity. In those cases, what is produced seems to be an act of "creation out of nothing," or at least something that springs

---

[1] For a convenient sampling of these cosmogonic myths, see Barbara C. Sproul, *Primal Myths: Creating the World* (New York: Harper and Row, 1979); Carmen Blacker and Michael Loewe, eds., *Ancient Cosmologies* (London: George Allen and Unwin, 1975); E. O. James, *Creation and Cosmology* (Leiden: E. J. Brill, 1969).

from the artist's mind. And one is not as prone to look for antecedent conditions to explain the spontaneous origination of genuinely creative ideas. For this reason, we may assume, art and creative craftsmanship become, at sophisticated levels of cosmogonic myth-making, preferred analogical sources for explaining the existence and structure of the world. As thoughtful beings eager to find explanations for even the most fundamental matters, we are drawn to understanding the existence and patterns of the world around us as the handiwork of a supremely wise and infinitely creative Designer and Maker of all things.

It is this fact that explains the powerful and not easily surrendered appeal of theism's doctrine of Creation. It is this component of theistic philosophy that, in our Western traditions, is worked out in Plato's *Timaeus* and by theologians of the Jewish, Christian, and Muslim religious faiths who, building on their Greek heritage, seek to coordinate the inherited insights and arguments of Greek philosophy with the narratives or revelations of their respective sacred, scriptural texts.

PLATO'S *TIMAEUS*

Plato's *Timaeus* is a clear and outstanding example of an entire class of creation myths that seek to answer, in their own way, the question of reality. For purposes of explaining the existence and fundamental pattern of the world and all that it contains, the generic characteristic of such myths is the appeal to a fundamental distinction between two levels or types of reality: the world or cosmos, on the one hand, and what lies "beyond" the world, on the other, yet whose properties and powers in relation to the world explain the reality of the latter as an ordered whole.

For Plato, reality consists basically of two tiers: one a domain of Intelligible Forms, the other a structured cosmos. His myth of creation would link the two through the agency of a Divine Craftsman who practices the rational art of cosmic ordering. In his creation myth, Plato achieved a degree of sophistication and plausibility far beyond anything found in primitive cosmogonies.

As a result, for those to whom in general the project of working out a cosmogony, whether in the form of a myth or through some other method, is the basic path to follow in achieving an answer to the question of reality, his views exerted, and continue to exert, a profound impact. To mention just two examples: it set the pattern for many of the details of later theology, and it offered a rationale for the activity of many scientists engaged in actual research. In the first case, unlike other tentative or partial parallels to and anticipations of later theism, Plato's *Timaeus* played a crucial role in guiding many of the central theological doctrines of later Jewish, Christian, and Muslim thought. And in the other direction, its influence is found in those philosophies of science that are commonly referred to as being *realist* in their outlook, and that would support the claim that the inherent structure of the world is essentially quantitative. Such views share with Plato a strong adherence to the Pythagorean heritage, a heritage that has been enormously enriched through the growth of modern mathematics and its manifold successful applications in science. This orientation finds encouragement in Plato's belief that the Divine Craftsman imposed (in addition to a teleological ordering) a determinate pattern of mathematical (particularly geometrical) intelligibility on Nature. As embedded in material things, this intelligible structure constitutes their objective essence.

Plato writes that "the world has been fashioned on the model of that which is comprehensible by rational discourse and understanding."[2] This brief statement sums up not only a crucial feature of Plato's own philosophy, but points ahead as a beacon in the history of Western thought that illuminates the common orientation of many subsequent versions of realist theories in ontology and epistemology, whether such realist doctrines are directly supportive of theism or even, as in the case of some naturalistic philosophies, in open rebellion against theism. One of my purposes, in what follows, is to review briefly the way in which the

[2] *Timaeus*, 29A, in *Plato's Cosmology*, trans. F. M. Cornford (London: Routledge and Kegan Paul, 1937).

realist approach to intelligibility was expounded in classic form in Plato's philosophy. The important idea I shall focus on is the belief that there is a single, definite, inherent intelligible order in the world, that it can be discovered by human beings, and that it owes its origin and existence to a transcendent Creative Source.

The use of the notion of *intelligibility* (or *intelligible structure*), as influenced by Plato's *Timaeus* and his other dialogues, has had a long career in the history of Western thought. It has been modified and adapted to serve various special interests: religious, scientific, and philosophic. Whether in ancient, medieval, or modern times, the vast majority of world views held by philosophers, theologians, scientists, and countless other individuals have been realist in their basic presuppositions and orientation. As commonly used in its broad philosophic meaning, realism is the fundamental and unquestioned belief in the existence of an independent reality that is made up of its own component entities, together with their inherent properties and structural interconnections. This reality is taken to exist apart from, and antecedently to, any human efforts to disclose what that reality is. For those who adopt this basic ontological commitment, it is commonly agreed, therefore, that the task of a sound method and trusted source of knowledge is to *discover*—to bring to light and articulate, as far as possible—the nature of this independently existing reality.

This shared realism holds for a broad spectrum of philosophic views. Each view may be radically or only partially different from another in drawing its own distinctive internal lines of differentiation with respect to the fundamental types, levels, and modes of being that identify the component entities that, for it, comprise independent reality. This common ontological realism is associated, moreover, with a wide range of epistemological approaches—for example, empiricist, rationalist, revelationist, fideist, mystical, or a mixture of some of these. A particular epistemological orientation and preference selects the mode of knowledge acquisition to be relied on in disclosing the nature of reality. The presupposition of realism accordingly underlies such diverse world views as theism, platonism, materialism, subjective idealism (mentalism), absolute idealism, and naturalism. It appears in such differently oriented thinkers as Plato, Aristotle, Plotinus, Augustine, Philo, Avicenna, Aquinas, Hobbes, Descartes, Spinoza, Leibniz, and Berkeley, among others. A paradigm of this realist philosophy—one that has exerted an enormous influence on various family-related versions of realism, even those ostensibly in opposition to it at various points—is the kind we find in Plato's myth of cosmic creation in the *Timaeus*.

In response to the perennial human need to understand the world and man's place in it, Plato's philosophy centers its attention on the role that *reason* performs in imposing (as far as is possible) a maximally satisfactory, rational order on given raw materials. I shall refer to this as Plato's emphasis on the general theme of *rational art*. As conveyed in his various *Dialogues*, Plato's philosophy may be viewed as an attempt to work out the details of this fundamental idea, and to show how its general principles could be applied in helping to find answers to such widely different questions as formulating a sound political philosophy, adopting a philosophy to guide one's personal life, and achieving a conception of the physical cosmos on its most comprehensive scale. In opposition to those who are either ignorant of these principles or deliberately flout them, Plato is at pains to make them explicit and to show that only if we accept these principles can we genuinely make sense both of what human life could accomplish, and of how, more broadly, we may find intelligibility in the existence and structure of the cosmos.

In its original meaning, the Greek term *kosmos* referred to adornment or order.[3] Its application by some Greek philosophers of the sixth century B.C. as a designation for the physical, visible universe as a whole was an innovative extension of this ordinary meaning. Plato takes advantage of this extension in making his

[3] Cf. Charles H. Kahn, *Anaximander and the Origins of Greek Cosmology*, Appendix 1, "The Usage of the Term KOSMOS in Early Greek Philosophy" (New York: Columbia University Press, 1960).

own comparisons between the kinds of order to be found both in the *microcosm* and the *macrocosm*. For example, in the *Republic*, Plato shows what a reliance on the principles of rational political art would require in establishing and managing a well-ordered (just) society, and, by way of analogy, what parallels this would have in the application of the same broad principles in achieving a well-ordered personal life. This two-tiered conception of a rational life for human beings (the political and the personal) constitutes Plato's conception of the *microcosm*, of what life would be like if practiced in accordance with rational art. His dialogue *Timaeus* explores the same underlying central, general idea of rational art as a way of coming to understand the *macrocosm*: the genesis and structure of the cosmos as a whole. In sharp opposition to the views of materialists (for example, Atomists such as Democritus), Plato is convinced that the universe displays the marks of being a well-ordered product of deliberate design: of rational art, not of chance.

For human beings, the achievement of a well-ordered personal life is the outcome of applying reason to a complex set of psychological and biological capacities, needs, and drives. In the case of envisioning what it would be like to have a well-ordered and just society, the problem is one of specifying the interrelations among the distinctive functions and contributions that different classes of society would make to the welfare of the society as a whole. Finally, in the case of the cosmos on its grandest scale, Plato believes that "the world is the best of things that have become,"[4] and that to understand what makes it a well-ordered, intelligible whole, it is best to conceive it as the handiwork of a Divine Artificer or Demiurge who imposed a rational structure on certain primordial, uncreated, unformed, physical materials. In each case, the result of rational art consists in the relatively successful application of reason to certain distinctive raw materials.

When comparing the structure of the macrocosm and the microcosm in the light of an emphasis on the notion of rational art,

---

[4] *Timaeus*, 29A.

and in finding that they share certain basic similarities, Plato makes use of what, for him, are a number of important basic principles. In the world at large, as well as in human life, no "craftsman," "maker," or "artist," whether rational or not, starts with a clean slate. In particular, any rational agent, human or divine, finds, inherits, or is confronted with certain given, raw materials. A second theme to which Plato devotes much attention is the nature of reason. Whether exemplified on a human or superhuman scale, the operation of reason, according to Plato, is grounded in absolute, infallible knowledge, not on blind (arbitrary) choice, custom, or variable opinions. The exercise of reason requires insight into or infallible knowledge of what exists independently of reason and is in this sense wholly objective. For Plato, this means having an unclouded access to the world of intelligible Forms. In contrast with the views of relativists (for example, the Sophists of his day), Plato maintains that the special virtue of the exercise of reason is wisdom: the choice and embodiment, as far as is possible, of what is absolutely true and good. Finally, Plato makes use of the combination of the foregoing principles in his account of what I have labeled "rational art." A mind, whether human or divine, possessed of reason and having infallible knowledge of the wholly perfect, unchanging, luminously intelligible domain of Ideal Forms, is able as a result to make wise choices in the effort to embody and apply one (or a combination) of those Forms in some given material not previously well ordered by rational art. However, no product of rational art in the domain of "becoming," even when successful, is perfect, everlasting, or totally rational. In any embodiment of rational art that results from "copying" ideal Forms, there is always a residual and uncontrollable element of recalcitrance, changeability, imperfection, transience, or "necessity" and chance (*ananke*) that persists. However, insofar as the product is one of rational art, there is in it an objectively existing, discoverable, intelligible order that was put there in the process of creation. The fruits of this rational art become accessible afterwards to anyone equipped with reason who examines and appreciates the work.

In the introductory conversation of the *Timaeus*, Plato sets the stage for the rest of the dialogue by calling upon Timaeus (a mouthpiece for Plato's own views), because "he knows more of astronomy than the rest of us and has made knowledge of the nature of the universe his chief object." In covering this theme, we are to expect that "he will begin with the birth of the world and end with the nature of man" (27A).

At the outset of his discourse, Timaeus makes the following remark: "I who speak and you my judges are only human, and consequently it is fitting that we should, in these matters, accept the likely story (*mythos*) and look for nothing further" (29C–D). Like everything else in this historically important and highly influential text, this sentence has been given many different interpretations. We need to pause at this point, therefore, to consider how we shall interpret this cautionary remark. Since there are many special topics covered in Timaeus's lengthy discourse, Plato's use of the expression *mythos*, here translated as "likely story," should be treated, I suggest, in different ways when applied to the different kinds of claims he puts forth at different stages in the development of the dialogue, or to different layers of the analysis. I suggest that we distinguish three such different (though related) types, degrees, or levels of insight and understanding. These, however, are not, in Plato's presentation, contained within sharply demarcated sections belonging to each in turn. Overlappings abound, and transitions are not abrupt.

At the very beginning, Timaeus (Plato) makes quite explicit and clear the basic philosophic presupposition that will govern his entire discussion.

> We must, then, in my judgment, first make this distinction: what is that which is always real and has no becoming, and what is that which is always becoming and is never real? That which is apprehensible by thought with a rational account is the thing that is always unchangeably real; whereas that which is the object of belief together with unreasoning sensation is the thing that becomes and passess away, but never has real being. [28A]

We may think of the statement of this fundamental presupposition as occupying a "first level" of discourse for the ensuing discussion. It underlies all phases of that discussion and is never abandoned or modified. It remains to the end a cornerstone of Plato's philosophical outlook. For Plato, the acceptance and articulation of this presupposition is in no way to be thought of as based on a "likely story" (*mythos*), if this is taken as allowing that the account to which this description is applied is a fiction or may be totally false. On the contrary, the statement of this presupposition, in its basic and general form, represents for Plato a fixed, certain, unshakable principle of his world view. It had this status for him throughout his life, even though at different stages of his intellectual development he recognized various problems connected with giving it an adequate, trouble-free formulation. He never ceased to struggle, therefore, to make it as clear and unobjectionable as possible, so that others, too, would be persuaded of the need to take it as the starting point of all philosophic inquiry.

On this first level of discourse, the basic ontological distinction Plato draws is between, on the one hand, the realm of eternal, perfect, uncreated, incorporeal, supra-sensible, fully intelligible Forms (what, in the context of Plato's philosophy, is referred to as the domain of Being), and, on the other, the domain of imperfect, changing, sensible, material entities and phenomena (the domain of Becoming). As possessed of perfect reality or Being and occupying their own fixed and independent status in reality, the Forms as such are not found in ordinary sensory experience or in any material objects: they are not located in space nor do they have any temporal duration, not even an everlasting one. In occupying their own highest degree or level of reality, Forms are accessible only to those equipped with reason. Any exemplification or instantiation of Forms is only a likeness (*eikon*) of that which is an unchanging model (*paradeigma*). At best and as a result of the practice of rational art, Forms may be exemplified or instantiated imperfectly and approximately in sensible and material entities, processes, or activities.

Since the Forms are eternal, unchanging, perfect, and wholly intelligible when considered distributively, for Plato they do not provoke the human need to *explain* their Being by reference to some more fundamental cause or agency. The situation, however, is quite different with respect to anything that belongs to the realm of material and sensible entities. "All that becomes must needs become by the agency of some cause; for without a cause nothing can come to be" (28A). In the case of material and sensible entities that belong to the domain of Becoming, we look for explanations: we seek to understand what brought them into existence and the reasons for the qualities or properties they possess.

With these distinctions in place, and in turning to the cosmos, Plato has no doubt about where to locate it in this overall ontological scheme:

> So concerning the whole Heaven or World—let us call it by whatsoever name may be most acceptable to it—we must ask the question which, it is agreed, must be asked at the outset of inquiry concerning anything: Has it always been, without any source of becoming; or has it come to be, starting from some beginning? It has come to be; for it can be seen and touched and it has body, and all such things are sensible; and, as we saw, sensible things, that are to be apprehended by belief together with sensation, are things that become and are generated.[5]

Having made this assignment of where the cosmos belongs in the fundamental, unquestioned ontological scheme with which he started, a number of consequences follow. In the first place, since by definition for Plato everything in the domain of sensible and material reality undergoes change ("becomes") and has a beginning or source (is "generated"), it follows that the material and sensible cosmos must also have some beginning or source, something to which it owes its existence and character. The existence

[5] *Timaeus*, 28C.

of the cosmos must also "become by the agency of some cause";[6] it cannot be left unexplained, a brute, wholly irrational datum. Why not? Plato's answer depends on our recalling that in referring to our world as a *cosmos*, we are referring not only to something that exists in a material and sensible way, and so belongs to the domain of Becoming, but also to something that has an order, a structure that can be understood. In using this description, we show our recognition of the fact that it is the kind of entity that is not chaotic or made up of random, chance, or accidental happenings. It displays various patterns of regularity and a manifold differentiation into objects, events, and processes that can be classified, predicted, and explained.

And here Plato makes a crucial assumption. If we are going to explain *this* aspect of the world—that it is ordered and intelligible in however limited a fashion—we must look beyond the sheer fact that it manifests multiplicity and change. Unlike materialism, naturalism, or other types of metaphysical schemes that do not look beyond the cosmos for the explanation of the order which it contains but, instead, accept it as a primordial, inherent, objective (realistic) feature of the world itself, Plato takes the existence of order in the world as something that calls for an explanation. It is not, for him, a primordial feature that serves to explain, derivatively, other features, while remaining unexplained in its own existence and presence. On the contrary, its presence calls for an explanation by reference to something of a more fundamental metaphysical character and status: it must be in some way a derivative feature of something more basic. And for Plato this "something more basic" is not to be found *in* the cosmos, but in some sense "beyond" it. It must be "supernatural."[7]

---

[6] *Timaeus*, 28C.

[7] Gregory Vlastos makes the point clearly: "What Heraclitus had denied when he wrote, 'this world, the same for all, no man or god has made,' Plato makes the first principle of cosmology in the *Timaeus*. He undertakes to depict the origin of the cosmos as the work of a god who takes over matter in a chaotic state and moulds it in the likeness of an ideal model, the Platonic Idea of Living Creature

Accordingly, in looking for a model on which to base an explanation of the existence of order in the cosmos Plato fastens, in the first place, on the familiar human practice of various arts and crafts. These obviously involve a type of activity in which order is deliberately and designfully introduced into some material by a properly trained or technically equipped agent. In his dialogue *Gorgias*, Plato had already pointed out this fundamental feature of art: "Look at artists, builders, shipwrights or followers of any other craft, how each of them imparts a certain arrangement to what he is working on, and makes one part fit and harmonize with another until he has constructed the whole as a thing of system and order" (503E–504B).

For Plato, the adoption of this model to guide our understanding of the source of order in the cosmos must nevertheless submit to certain appropriate modifications. As contrasted with ordinary arts and crafts in which a craftsman introduces a design into his raw materials that is based either on tradition and prevailing accepted styles, or on idiosyncratic personal (subjective) inspiration, imagination, or technical ingenuity, the rational art of cosmogony is based on the appeal to absolute, fixed, objective, universal, rationally discoverable, ideal standards. In accordance with the basic commitments of Plato's ontology, the satisfaction of this latter requirement is made possible by a mind that has supreme rational access to the domain of Forms where intelligibility *par excellence* is to be found. In that domain, everything is luminously intelligible to reason. If what exists on the level of Becoming, too, is found to display some evidence of the presence of intelligible structure, this could only come about by the action of some mechanism or bridge that is able to bring aspects of the intelligibility of Forms into the realm of Becoming. In short, there must be some causal link that imports or copies the feature of intelli-

---

(30C ff.) That this god is supernatural in the literal sense of the term is plain enough: he stands outside of nature and above it; he is not himself a member of the system of interacting entities which constitutes nature; he acts upon that system, but the system does not act upon him." *Plato's Universe* (Seattle: University of Washington Press, 1975), 25.

gibility inherent in the domain of Forms and embodies it in some degree in the otherwise unformed domain of Becoming. As a result of this copying (of bringing about an instantiation or exemplification of Forms in the domain of Becoming), the accessibility to and reliance on the intelligibility of Forms is shown to be a necessary condition for the possibility of having an intelligible cosmos.

Plato goes further. According to him, the only kind of cause that can accomplish this transfer of intelligibility is a rational agent, a conscious being that has at least a threefold set of powers. First, it has the power of conscious, rational apprehension of the domain of Forms. Second, it has the power to bring about (at least with some degree of success) a transference of the intelligibility inherent in Forms into the otherwise wholly unintelligible domain of brute, chaotic, chance happenings. The two aforementioned powers belong to the type of agent we can classify as a "craftsman," a "maker." However, a third feature must be added if we are going to use the model of craftsmanship to account for the discovered order of the cosmos.

> Let us, then, state for what reason becoming and this universe were framed by him who framed them. He was good; and in the good no jealousy in any matter can ever arise. So, being without jealousy, he desired that all things should come as near as possible to being like himself. That this is the supremely valid principle of becoming and of the order of the world, we shall most surely be right to accept from men of understanding. Desiring, then, that all things should be good and, so far as might be, nothing imperfect, the god took over all that is visible—not at rest, but in discordant and unordered motion—and brought it from disorder into order, since he judged that order was in every way the better.[8]

In the light of Plato's stress on this third factor, the discoverable intelligibility and order of the cosmos is not, for example (as the

---

[8] *Timaeus*, 29D–30A.

Pythagoreans had stressed), simply a matter involving the successful use of mathematics to discern structure in the motions and arrangements of material bodies. It may be that, too, but it is also one of recognizing a purposeful design directed to the achievement of desirable and beneficent ends. The cosmos is not only mathematically but also teleologically intelligible. Accordingly, since the cosmos is well ordered, it requires the kind of agent that is conscious, capable of intelligent design, benevolently inclined, and has sufficient power to accomplish the transformation of given unformed materials into the finished product that we find. It must have sufficient (but not unlimited) power, since, like all craftsmen, it does not have complete control: it must work with the materials or medium it starts with. Another way of making this point is to recognize that in his appeal to the notion of creation or craftsmanship for his cosmogony, and in contrast to later theological views, Plato does not subscribe to a theory of creation *ex nihilo*.

Plato attributes these three characteristics (of rational apprehension, transformative power over raw materials, and beneficent concern with realizing the maximum possible goodness) to the Divine Artificer who practiced the principles of rational art on its most comprehensive scale—cosmogony—to produce a well-ordered cosmos. The well-orderedness could not be explained as arising either by chance or by the actions of a "crafty," malevolent intelligence. Having convinced himself that there is a rational agent who is the maker and father of the universe, Plato affirms his belief that "the world is the best of things that have become. . . . Having come to be, then, in this way, the world has been fashioned on the model of that which is comprehensible by rational discourse and understanding and is always in the same state."[9]

While convinced there is a rational agent that produced order in the cosmos and made it intelligible, Plato admits that he has no way of specifying, with any great detail, further characteristics of this agent. "The Maker and Father of this Universe is hard to

[9] *Timaeus*, 29A.

find, and when found, impossible to describe to all and sundry."[10] As evidence of this uncertainty and limited insight, Plato uses a variety of expressions to refer to this rational agent of cosmogonic range and power. Frequently he uses the term *theos*, accompanied by the definite article (therefore to be translated "God," in distinction from references to subordinate gods), alongside such other expressions as "Maker," "Father," and "Demiurge" (*demiourgos*, craftsman).[11] Whatever name is used, however, Plato can only be sure of his "true belief" *that* the cosmogonic agent exists, not of any precise knowledge of *what* the exact nature of the agent is.

Is, then, this conviction of Plato to be classified as a *mythos*, a likely story? In reply, it would be useful to distinguish, in the first place, the way in which this description could be applied to Plato's account of the existence of a Divine Artificer, as compared to the status Plato assigns to the principle of ontological dualism (the basic distinction between Being and Becoming he enunciated at the outset of the dialogue). For Plato, that there is a Rational Agent who established the order of the cosmos is a deep conviction. However, it is not a conviction he is prepared to articulate in any great detail. It has something in common with the basic philosophic presupposition of ontological dualism concerning the domains of Being and Becoming, previously referred to. Like the commitment to the latter principle, the belief in a Rational Cosmogonic Craftsman is also, for Plato, a matter of unshakable conviction, a matter of basic philosophic "faith." For Plato, one might say, this is the way reality is, and he is simply

[10] *Timaeus*, 28C, in W.K.C. Guthrie, *A History of Greek Philosophy*, vol. 5 (Cambridge, Eng.: Cambridge University Press, 1978), 255.

[11] We must admit, however, that of all the images used, those associated with the model of Craftsmanship have a certain primacy and predominance in Plato's account. It is this model that encourages the use of such metaphors as "moulding," "cutting up," "measuring out," "pouring into a mixing bowl," "splicing together," among others, that one finds, for example, in the account of how the Demiurge came to assign the several patterns of celestial motions to the various heavenly bodies (the "rational soul" of the cosmos). Cf. Vlastos, *Plato's Universe*, 26.

declaring what he "finds" it to be at bottom. However, the defense of it, its articulation and support, cannot be carried out at this level with proofs, arguments, or detailed appeals to common observational experience. Whatever articulation he gives can only be accomplished with the aid of analogy, myth, metaphor, and a sense of its general consonance with his other basic ontological convictions.

Yet Plato does go further as he continues in the elaboration of his cosmogonic myth. That myth, based on the metaphor or model of craftsmanship, requires as its chief components (1) a Maker (the Demiurge); (2) a Rational Plan or model (obtained from the domain of Forms); (3) unformed material (a preexistent, "given" or "found" medium) in which to realize the model; and (4) the finished product (the cosmos). We have considered briefly, thus far, Plato's appeal to the intelligible domain of Forms as the source of the Demiurge's model, and the kind of language Plato uses in referring to the Maker. It remains also to briefly consider the way in which Plato treats the other two components (the "raw material" and the "finished product") in his use of the underlying imagery of the model of craftsmanship. The first leads us to his discussion of what he calls "the Receptacle," the second to his description of the cosmos as "a Living Creature possessed of a Body and Soul."

In describing the material or medium into which the Demiurge, with the aid of a model, introduces the features of a rationally apprehended Form, Plato once again resorts to various images and metaphoric descriptions. These are not to be taken literally, and indeed—because of the differences in the sources of human experience from which they are analogically borrowed—they are not totally consistent with one another. For example, the "material medium" is described in language borrowed from animal and human sexual reproduction and generation. The recipient material is compared to the Mother (although, less appropriately, also to a Nurse). In describing the Mother's role, the Recipient is referred to as providing the "receptacle" (womb) in which the cosmos is nourished. In conformity with general Greek conceptions of his day, Plato identifies the sole (cosmic) generator with the Father. Their offspring, of course, is the cosmos, a Living Creature. In addition to the foregoing metaphors, Plato compares the primordial Receptacle to a smooth material such as gold or wax on which particular patterns can be impressed without obtruding any qualities of its own, or to the oil that serves as the neutral base for perfumes. Again, Plato ascribes to the Receptacle the properties of Space, both in the sense of pure extension, but also in the sense of being constituted by the pervasive presence of irregular, agitated motions of various rudimentary powers and qualities. In the latter sense, Space is a primordial, not wholly eliminable manifestation of Necessity (*ananke*)—or, what for the Greeks amounts to the same thing, of Chance—"before" Reason gets to work in "persuading it to receive" (to some extent) a pattern of regularity for its contents and motions.[12]

Plato's reliance on the basic model of craftsmanship supports, among other things, his conviction that the cosmos is unique and finite. He differs here from the atomists and other pre-Socratics who had speculated on the existence of a possibly infinite plurality of coexisting or successive "worlds" in an infinite universe. Just as a human craftsman produces a work of his art that is finite, not infinite, so too the Divine Craftsman, in fashioning the world into a cosmos, gave it a finitely extended structure, at least spatially. Indeed, Plato conceives of the structure of the finite cosmos as that of a comprehensive Living Creature, endowed with a Cosmic Rational Soul joined to its Cosmic Body (30B). The

[12] This latter conception of Space has fascinating resonances with some recent discussions in cosmology and particle physics. For example, the program of geometrodynamics, developed by John Wheeler and his co-workers, as a way of approaching the main ideas of general relativity theory, can be examined in this way. Similarly, recent quantum field theories and other ventures in particle physics that make use of the notion of the vacuum also have an uncanny family resemblance to some of the things Plato says about the Receptacle. For a discussion of the Platonic background to geometrodynamics, see John C. Graves, *The Conceptual Foundations of Contemporary Relativity Theory* (Cambridge, Mass.: The MIT Press, 1971), especially chap. 5 and Foreword by John A. Wheeler); also, on the vacuum, see my *Cosmic Understanding*, chap. 4.

Living Creature that is the cosmos includes all other living creatures. The latter comprise four major groups: (1) the created, subordinate, living gods that animate the stars, planets, and the Earth; (2) land-based animals; (3) fish; and (4) birds. The model for the Cosmic Living Creature, Plato claims, was itself a unique Intelligible Form, selected by the Demiurge from the entire domain of Intelligible Forms.

> What was the living creature in whose likeness he framed the world? We must not suppose that it was any creature that ranks only as a species; for no copy of that which is incomplete can ever be good. Let us rather say that the world is like, above all things, to that Living Creature of which all other living creatures, severally and in their families, are parts. For that embraces and contains within itself all the intelligible living creatures just as this world contains ourselves and all other creatures that have been formed as things visible. For the god, wishing to make this world most nearly like that intelligible thing which is best and in every way complete, fashioned it as a single visible living creature, containing within itself all living things whose nature is of the same order. [30C–31]

Thus far, Plato's account of cosmogony has been conducted on what I suggest we think of as its first and second levels of analysis. Although partially different from one another, as previously pointed out, the account on these two levels constitutes a statement of Plato's philosophic faith. In carrying out the analysis of his model of Divine Craftsmanship, especially, Plato makes extensive use of metaphors. And he would be the first to admit that although his underlying purpose and commitment are to be taken seriously and literally, the way in which he conveys his convictions here, on the second level, is, through the language of myth, a "likely story."

In further elaboration of his cosmogonic myth, Plato speculates, for example, that the Demiurge created various subordinate gods in order to help in carrying out the designs of the Divine

Artificer. This, along with other similar speculations, represent at best an exercise in myth making. These details belong to what I here think of as belonging to the second level of discourse in the *Timaeus*. It is only a likely story. Its details are to be accepted as only an exercise of analogy and imagination. But the underlying premise on which this analogy is grounded—that there must be a cause for the existence and structure of the cosmos—this, for Plato, is not a likely matter; it is not a conviction he would be prepared to surrender. Hence the likely story that characterizes the cosmogony in its most general characteristics is a mixture: part fancy, part deep conviction, or what Plato takes to be true belief. Plato would not be prepared to abandon the deep conviction or true belief (the "faith" part). However, we may suppose, he would be fully ready to admit that the imaginative details he introduces in order to fill out the account of the craftsman analogy make up only a myth, a reasonable and helpful story, no more than that. It is to be taken by intelligent readers with a grain of salt, with deference to the limits of human powers of understanding and explanation. The improvement on this story is not a matter of increasing its probability and improving its closeness to the truth and therefore something to be left to further inquiry and science. For on this level we are dealing with questions that cannot be answered fully, or in some gradual, progressively improving way, by science.

However, there is a third level of analysis yet to come and it occupies a long and detailed section of the dialogue. In it, Plato gives his account of the properties of the created cosmos, from its most inclusive and comprehensive scale down to the level of the workings of its varied inner contents. The cosmos can be roughly divided into the astronomical domain of celestial motions, the physico-chemical domain of the primary, elementary material constituents of all bodies in the cosmos, and finally the biological domain of all living creatures, culminating with human beings. The astronomy describes the central position of the Earth in the cosmos, the shape and motion of the cosmos as a whole, together with the distinctive yet interrelated motions of the Sun, Moon, planets, and fixed stars. The section dealing with the physics and chemistry of elementary particles undertakes to describe and explain how they came to be, what their different types are, and how they form the basis of all sensible, material, gross entities. The biological section deals with all types of living creatures whether land-based, aquatic, or aerial (whether endowed with rational souls or not), and with the major features that explain the physiological (including medically relevant) aspects and psychological properties of the human animal. All of this Plato works out with considerable, ingenious detail, relying not only on his own creative and imaginative powers as a proto-scientist, but by incorporating the theories of the Pythagoreans, atomists, and other scientists and mathematicians of his day. All of this encyclopedic summary of factual detail belongs to the level of what we should recognize as the kinds of interests that scientists have.

On this third (protoscientific) level, Plato offers particular descriptive and explanatory theories of specific natural phenomena. His account involves geometry, relies on observational details, and displays great ingenuity in the construction of theories. With the enormous advances of science since Plato's day, one can no longer take seriously the bulk of this material, although one can continue to study it with great admiration and interest.[13] It is a reasonable inference that Plato would admit that these descriptions and explanations are "likely stories" in the sense of belonging to a probable *logos*. He would say this with full recognition that they represent only his (and some of his contemporaries') best efforts at understanding the detailed mechanisms of the observable world. One may suppose he would be the first to admit their comparative inadequacy, and would abandon his own accounts or that of his colleagues operating on the same level, if we could imagine him being transported to our own day and confronted with the best available discoveries and theories of contemporary science. His likely stories are only the first primitive steps on the long road to increasing, refining, and improving our hu-

---

[13] For an account of this material, see Vlastos, *Plato's Universe.*

man understanding of the world's detailed structure. Even if more recent stories are themselves only probable or likely, they are better than his own likely story in astronomy or the other sciences. Yet, when taken together, they represent steps toward the goal of ultimately disclosing the intelligible structure that the cosmos possesses as a result of the Demiurge's practice of the rational art of cosmogony.

To sum up: For Plato, the first level of discourse is a fixed, certain, commitment. The second level is a mixture of commitment and imagination. The third is a tentative exercise in progressive inquiry. He would not surrender what he says on the first level. He would acknowledge the imaginative part of the second level, but would not surrender the component of deep conviction that the cosmos is the product of rational art. His acceptance of the account given on the third level is also seriously intended, although he would admit its truth is only tentative: it could be challenged and overthrown by better information, observation, and scientific theories.

Plato's account of the overall nature of science as a multifaceted project of discovering the intelligible structure of the cosmos has been a paradigm for other attempts to describe the nature of scientific activity and its goals, even though (over the centuries and as a result of manifold changes in the discoveries and content of science) scientists and philosophers of science have found it necessary to modify Plato's original formulations and emphases.

Thus in Aristotle, the use of the notion of intelligibility was given a central place in his own system of thought. However, for Aristotle this involved disengaging it from Plato's espousal of the underlying scheme of ontological dualism with its adherence to the conception of the domain of perfect Intelligible Forms as wholly distinct from the domain of material and sensible entities, and the use of this doctrine in the cosmogonic myth of the *Timaeus*. For Aristotle, intelligibility is a discoverable, objective, and inherent set of properties belonging to objects and events. It is accessible to properly exercised inquiries by human reason (*nous*). Intelligibility is to be found directly in Nature, not via apprehension of its ideal models in the world of Forms. Intelligibility is to be found in the physical cosmos and in all types of natural substances. Aristotle's account of substance was strongly influenced by his own detailed and elaborate investigations of living things. His biologically oriented taxonomic interests (in genera and species, and in individual substances exemplifying generic characteristics) provided him with standard examples of intelligibility.

With the emergence of science in the modern era, already well under way by the seventeenth century, return to the notion of intelligibility, as stressed in Aristotle's philosophy of science, was given a new articulation. Instead of Aristotle's biologically influenced taxonomic models of intelligibility, emphasis was increasingly placed on the notions of empirically established and mathematically expressed laws. This new emphasis was especially seen in physics, astronomy, and chemistry through the work of such investigators as Galileo, Descartes, Kepler, and Boyle. Their achievements served to support the latest transformation and modification of the Platonic notion of objective intelligibility. In their own philosophic interpretation of these scientific achievements, many scientists and philosophers showed the influence of the Pythagorean side of Plato's philosophy as distinguished from its teleological side. They readily found support for this emphasis as a result of the central role mathematics plays in physics and astronomy.

These philosophies have been largely successful in demolishing the belief that the world was designed and regulated by a beneficent Cosmic Creator through the agency of an externally imposed divine plan and by the workings of a multiform interlocking network of final causes. All the discoveries and theories of modern astronomy, scientific cosmology, and biological theories of evolution have joined to undermine a belief that the world is governed by laws imposed at creation in order to support the achievement of man's well-being.

Nevertheless, however successful the modern revolt against this major strand of a telelogically guaranteed anthropocentrism has been, it has left largely untouched another crucial component in the creational world view: the belief in the existence of a unique, independent, inherently objective, intelligible mathematico-causal structure in the world. This belief is still retained as a cardinal component of the world view of many philosophers, scientists, and laymen. It is adhered to even by many who would otherwise disassociate themselves from a broadly conceived theistic outlook. The emphasis among modern philosophies of science, as we see it, for example, in leading thinkers of the seventeenth century, is on the notion that science is engaged in uncovering the inherent, objective laws of nature, and that, for this purpose, it needs to assign a preferential role to the *primary qualities* (geometric facts about bodies and their motions), as contrasted with their *secondary qualities* (for example, color, sound, and taste). All this marks the implementation of Plato's thesis that the Demiurge imposed a mathematically intelligible order on the world at its creation.

In seeking for metaphors of cosmic scope to convey this emphasis, and in contrast with Plato's image of God as a craftsman whose handiwork is a Living Creature with Body and Soul, many modern thinkers appealed to the image of God as an author who created a Book of Nature. Galileo gave celebrated expression to this metaphor:

> Philosophy [natural philosophy] is written in this grand book, the universe, which stands continually open to our gaze. But the book cannot be understood unless one first learns to comprehend the language and read the letters in which it is composed. It is written in the language of mathematics, and the characters are triangles, circles, and other geometric figures without which it is humanly impossible to understand a single word of it; without these one wanders about in a dark labyrinth.[14]

[14] Galileo, *The Assayer*, trans. Stillman Drake (New York: Doubleday Anchor Books, 1957), 237–238. On Galileo's use of the imagery of "the book of nature"

A further clear example of the influence of the mathematical orientation to understanding the world, as Plato had stressed, is to be found in Kepler's oft-stated and acknowledged Platonism. He makes clear his great indebtedness to Plato's *Timaeus* and to the work of the neo-Platonist Proclus in the latter's *Commentary on the First Book of Euclid's Elements*. Indeed, in a marginal note to a quotation from Proclus that Kepler cites, he makes the following remark with respect to the *Timaeus*: "[This is to be found] in *Timaeus*, which is beyond all possible doubt, a commentary on the book of Genesis, otherwise the first book of Moses, transforming it into Pythagorean philosophy, as will easily be apparent to an attentive reader who compares it with Moses' own words."[15] The Platonism of Kepler's thought is especially prominent in his two major cosmological works, the *Mysterium Cosmographicum* (1596) and *Harmonices Mundi Libri V* (1619), which came to him filtered through the neo-Platonism of Proclus, and as incorporated in Christian theology: "[I]n both works Kepler sets out to describe the beautiful Archetype according to which the observable Universe was constructed. Substituting the Christian God for Plato's gods and demiurges as the power behind the creative process appears to raise no problems. . . ."[16]

as well as its use by others, see Pietro Redondi, *Galileo: Heretic* (Princeton, N.J.: Princeton University Press, 1987), 37, fn. 14.

[15] *Harmonices Mundi*, Book IV, chap. 1, quoted in J. V. Field, *Kepler's Geometrical Cosmology* (Chicago: University of Chicago Press, 1988), 1. As Field points out, p. 220, the opinion that the *Timaeus* is a commentary on *Genesis* can be traced back to Philo Judaeus of Alexandria (fl. A.D. 40).

[16] Field, *Kepler*, 167. In his *Harmonices Mundi* (Augsburg, 1619) Kepler writes: "The Christians know that the mathematical principles according to which the corporeal world was to be created are coeternal with God; that God is soul and mind in the most supernally true sense of the word; and that human souls are images of God the Creator, conforming to Him in essentials as well. . . . Geometry is coeternal with the Mind of God before the creation of things; it is *God Himself* (what is in God that is not God Himself?) and has supplied God with the models for the creation of the world. With the image of God it has passed into man, and was certainly not received within through the eyes." See Book IV, quoted in Wolfgang Pauli, "The Influence of Archetypal Ideas on the Scientific

The same emphasis on the role of mathematical as well as causal analysis in making Nature intelligible was given a central position in the naturalistic philosophy of Spinoza. His realistic conception of intelligibility as that which preexists inquiry and belongs independently to Nature, yet is made explicit and given articulation by science, has remained the working philosophy and basic faith of very many scientists down to our own day. A prominent and clear example is the philosophy of Albert Einstein. His adherence to a type of Spinozism (despite his occasional appeals to certain Kantian ideas concerning the creative role of human scientific intelligence) belongs to this same broad Platonic heritage.[17]

The Platonic orientation to intelligibility, along with its many offshoots and descendants, is a heritage that has been challenged and, for many, largely replaced by taking seriously the kinds of insights stressed by Kant, the logical positivists, pragmatists, relativists, Wittgenstein, and others who in one way or another sought to overturn the realism of the Platonic approach to intelligibility. Later, we shall explore some of the details of this rival

---

Theories of Kepler," in C. G. Jung and W. Pauli, *The Interpretation of Nature and the Psyche* (London: Routledge and Kegan Paul, 1955), 164, 166.

[17] For a discussion of Einstein's Spinozism, see my book *Space, Time, and Creation: Philosophical Aspects of Scientific Cosmology* (New York: Free Press, 1957), chap. 7, sec. 2. Three weeks before Einstein's death, I had the privilege of having a private conversation with him, in which he responded to the critical remarks offered in my book and defended the importance to him as a scientist of retaining his Spinozist outlook.

Here, for example, is a recent statement of this type of philosophy: "Albert Einstein once said, 'I want to know how God created this world. I am not interested in this or that phenomenon, in the spectrum of this and that element. I want to know His thoughts, the rest are details.'

As a physicist, I am much enamoured of the sentiment expressed by Einstein. While the vast majority of contemporary physicists are engaged in explaining specific phenomena, and rightly so, a small group, the intellectual descendants of Einstein, have become more ambitious. They have entered the forest of the night in search of the fundamental design of Nature and, in their limitless hubris, have claimed to have glimpsed it." See A. Zee, *Fearful Symmetry: The Search for Beauty in Modern Physics* (New York: Macmillan Publishing Co., 1986), xi.

tradition and note its important repercussions on metaphysical efforts in answering the question of reality.

CREATION AND NOTHING

Plato's conception of the nature of reality, and its attendant treatment of the notion of intelligibility, has had a major influence throughout history not only on the way many scientists and philosophers of science have sought to interpret what it is that science seeks to accomplish, but also on the efforts of theologians and metaphysicians to formulate an answer to a quite different sort of question: the question commonly referred to as "the mystery of existence."[18]

Creational metaphysics and theologies of all varieties, despite their many differences, may be looked upon as so many attempts to answer the question of reality when this is expressed in the form "Why does the universe (cosmos, world) exist?" Many would agree with Leibniz and Heidegger that the question "Why is there Something rather than Nothing?" is the most fundamental question of all. They would regard the existence of the world as something calling for an explanation. Those closely identified with this broad orientation, and especially those imbued with a sense of this mystery as cultivated in theistic religion, believe it is the function of metaphysics or theology to examine the different ways in which the question may be asked, to study the answers that have been given, to consider the extent to which the question can be answered, and to decide whether to come to the realization that there may be no adequate human answer possible at all.

Our previous summary of Plato's myth of cosmic creation showed its place within his general conception of reality. Part of Plato's answer to the question of reality consisted in his defense

[18] For an analysis of the varied uses of this expression, see my book, *The Mystery of Existence* (New York: Appleton-Century-Crofts, 1965; reprinted, New York: New York University Press, 1974).

49

of the theory of Forms, a theory that stresses the existence of abstract entities that enjoy their own independent and genuine mode of nonphysical reality. Plato, however, believed there is more to reality than the domain of Forms and a disordered flux of physical existents; he believed in the existence of a Designing Intelligence whose operation transforms the disordered flux into a cosmos. The existence of the cosmos, metaphysically, is the product of the art of cosmic creation practiced by a Demiurge. Although Plato disclaimed any secure knowledge of the demiurgic agent, he was content to affirm his belief in his existence and activity, and to fill out some of the details of that activity partly by means of a myth and partly by means of a geometric theory of the fundamental elements of matter.

The theistic metaphysics of Judaism, Christianity, and Islam appropriated many of Plato's conceptual distinctions and shared in Plato's efforts at explaining the existence of the world as an ordered whole. Thus, with respect to some of the fundamental conceptual distinctions made by Plato, the conception of intelligibility as linked to and derived from a domain of Forms was given a central role in the theology of Philo Judaeus of Alexandria, St. Augustine, and the Church Fathers. For example, Philo Judaeus construed the domain of Intelligible Forms not as uncreated entities enjoying their own independent, eternal reality apart from God, as in Plato, but as *thoughts* in the mind of God, serving in this capacity as models for the creation of the world.[19]

Though such important modifications in and adaptations of Plato's cosmogonic myth were made by traditional theology in the process of working out the details of a theory of cosmic creation, there was one major point on which orthodox Jewish, Christian, and Muslim theologians united in opposition to Plato's account of cosmic creation. For Plato, the role of the Demiurge was modeled on human craftsmanship. A craftsman,

---

[19] See H. A. Wolfson, *Philo: Foundations of Religious Philosophy in Judaism, Christianity, and Islam* (Cambridge, Mass.: Harvard University Press, 1947), vol. I, chap. 4.

whether human or divine, confronts preexistent, given materials and imposes a new form on them; creation is a matter of transformation. A crucial thesis of orthodox schools of Jewish, Christian, and Muslim theology centered on a belief in creation *ex nihilo* and a rejection of the notion of uncreated matter. God's essence may be basically unknowable, but this much is known: everything that exists other than God owes its existence to God.

Thus, both Plato and traditional theology agreed in regarding the *existence of the world as an ordered structure* as something that calls for an *explanation*. In their respective explanations, both Plato and traditional theists adhered to a form of what, in the later history of philosophy, came to be called "the Principle of Sufficient Reason."[20] Both Plato and the traditional theist find this sufficient reason in the existence and activity of a Divine Maker of the world. Where they differ is in their application of this principle. For Plato, it is the observed and intelligible *order*

---

[20] A classic statement of the Principle of Sufficient Reason is given by Gottfried Wilhelm von Leibniz (1646–1716) in his work *The Principles of Nature and of Grace, Based on Reason* [1714], sec. 7: "[N]ow we must advance to *metaphysics*, making use of the *great principle*, little employed in general, which teaches that *nothing happens without a sufficient reason*; that is to say, that nothing happens without its being possible for him who should sufficiently understand things, to give a reason sufficient to determine why it is so and not otherwise. This principle laid down, the first question which should rightly be asked, will be, *Why is there something rather than nothing?* For nothing is simpler and easier than something. Further, suppose that things must exist, we must be able to give a reason *why they must exist so* and not otherwise.

"Now this sufficient reason for the existence of the universe cannot be found *in the series of contingent things*, that is, of bodies and of their representations in souls; for matter being indifferent in itself to motion and to rest, and to this or another motion, we cannot find the reason of the motion in it, and still less of a certain motion. And although the present motion which is in matter, comes from the preceding motion, and that from still another preceding, yet in this way we make no progress, go as far as we may; for the same question always remains. Thus it must be that the sufficient reason, which has no need of another reason, be outside this series of contingent things and be found in a substance which is its cause, or which is a necessary being, carrying the reason of its existence within itself; otherwise we should still not have a sufficient reason in which we could rest. And this final reason of things is called *God*."

in the world that calls for explanation. And he finds this explanation by saying its existence is the result of the activity of a Cosmic Craftsman who introduces order into "previously found" primordial, unordered raw materials. With the traditional theist, however, it is not only the order of the world that calls for explanation but the very *existence* of the world. Therefore, even the existence of the "raw materials" must be explained, not merely the order in the finished product. The theist makes use of the notion of creation *ex nihilo* to explain both the existence *of* and the structure *in* the world. Thus, although we can use the same phrase, "the existence of the world as ordered," as the common subject matter calling for explanation according to both Plato and the traditional theist, each relies on a different focus of emphasis in applying the term "exists." In Plato's case, "exists" attaches, as it were, to the fact *that there is an order*. In the case of the theist, the focus of the term "exists" is upon the world: *that there is a world*. While cosmic intelligibility for the theist is a twofold matter—of the intelligibility *that* there is a world at all, and that there is a discoverable, intelligible order in the world—for Plato the primary emphasis with respect to cosmic intelligibility is a single fact: that there is an intelligible order inherent in the world.

The belief not only in cosmic creation, but also the need to invoke the concept of "nothing," is consequently a distinctive feature of Western theology, whether orthodox or deviant. We face, therefore, the question of what to make of this concept of "nothing." Should it be included in our own conception of reality? Have the theistic schemes, whatever else they claimed, brought to light something of metaphysical importance? If one abandons the notion of cosmic creation, would this also entail an abandonment of the concept of "nothing"?

In my own choices for the direction in which to look in order to "answer the question of reality," and to which the present phase of my analysis is simply a historical preamble, I shall undertake to make sense of the proposal that the concept of "nothing" be salvaged, reinterpreted, and given an important role to perform in one's metaphysics. In making such use of this concept for present constructive metaphysical purposes, while pruning it of unwanted associations (including, along with other unwanted asociations, that it be understood as referring to a spatial Void), I shall relabel it "Boundless Existence." When the term "nothing" is understood in the special sense to be assigned to this expression—a sense I shall later clarify—I propose that we should be able to say "Boundless Existence is nothing." When so understood, Boundless Existence can be recognized as being a fundamental aspect of reality "beyond" that of the universe.

One of the great merits of traditional theism, in struggling to incorporate its own version of the notion of "nothing" in its metaphysical views, was a recognition of this aspect of reality. However, although my own constructive proposals for an acceptable metaphysics excludes appeal to the notion of cosmic creation—when this is thought of in connection with the activity of a transcendent, designing Creator or Demiurge—that metaphysics does include reference to the transcendent reality of Boundless Existence. I should maintain that an awareness of this dimension of reality is available to human beings apart from any adherence to a theistic creational metaphysics. By way of preparation for describing this type of awareness and the philosophic considerations that lead to its cultivation and exercise, it will be helpful to study its adumbration within the general framework of a creational metaphysics. Toward this end, I shall turn first to a brief review of certain deviant forms of religious thought, especially those associated with certain trends of mysticism in Judaism and Christianity.

Whatever their individually different degrees of affinity to many of Plato's doctrines, the Church Fathers were unanimous in their judgment that even if God created the world out of preexistent matter (as Plato claimed), this matter, too, was created by God. In short, they rejected the notion of an uncreated, eternal, preexistent matter.[21] Similarly, in the orthodox rabbinic tradition

---

[21] Cf. H. A. Wolfson, "Plato's Pre-existent Matter in Patristic Philosophy," in

of Judaism, from its earliest days, the Talmudic sages unanimously rejected the notion of an uncreated matter existing independently and coeternally with God and out of which God created the world. Representative of this view is the report of the following incident:

> A certain philosopher once raised the following question before Rabban Gamaliel, saying to him: "Your God was a great Artist, but He had at His disposal fine ingredients to help him." The (Patriarch) asked him: "What were they?" The philosopher replied: "*Tohu* and *Bohu* [usually rendered: 'without form and void'] and darkness and water and wind and deeps." Said Rabban Gamaliel to him: "Perish the thought! creation is stated in respect of all of them." [*Gen. Rabba* i, 4, p. 8][22]

In this reply there is a clear rejection of the conception of the creation of the world out of uncreated matter.

The conception of emanation, as developed by neo-Platonist metaphysics, was another type of view of the relation between the cosmos and ultimate reality rejected by those who adhered to an orthodox interpretation of creation. Typical of these views, and having the greatest influence, was the position of Plotinus.

In Plato there is a celebrated passage in which he compares the Form of the Good to the Sun.[23] Just as the latter casts its light on all things within its range, so the source of illumination for all other Forms in the "intelligible world," and hence for the human effort to make all things intelligible, is the Form of the Good. Plotinus uses this and other metaphors in his *Enneads*, where he describes the relation of the One—Ultimate, Primal Reality—and all other "lesser" or "derivative" levels of being.

Studies in the History of Philosophy and Religion (Cambridge, Mass.: Harvard University Press, 1973), vol. I, 175.

[22] E. E. Urbach, *The Sages*, trans. I. Abrahams (Cambridge, Mass: Harvard University Press, 1987), 188.

[23] Plato, *Republic*, vi, 508.

Existing beyond and above Being, It must be beyond and above Act, Mind or Intellection. That only can be named the Good to which all is bound and Itself to none. It must be unmoved while all circles around It, as a circumference around a centre from which all the radii proceed. Another example would be the sun, central to the light which streams from it and is yet linked to it; try as you will to separate the sun from its light, for ever the light is connected with the sun. [I, vii, 1]

Imagine a spring that has no source outside itself; it gives itself to all the rivers, yet never is exhausted by what they take, but remains quietly at rest; the tides that proceed from it are one within it before they run their several ways.

Or think of the life coursing throughout some mighty tree while yet it is the stationary principle of the whole; it is the giver of the entire and manifold life of the tree, but remains unmoved itself, not manifold, but the principle of that manifold life. [III, 8, 10][24]

At the heart of these and other metaphors used in an emanationist metaphysics is the conception of the One as the source or ground of all secondary, derivative, or lesser levels of reality. Yet because of the metaphors used in understanding their relation, those who adhered to this world view did not draw the kind of distinctions with respect to the meaning of "source" or "ground" that would have been acceptable to those upholding a strictly creational view. For from the perspective of the latter philosophy, emanationism leads to pantheism, a failure to draw the necessary distinctions between God and his creation. According to those upholding a creational theistic metaphysics, the world was created out of nothing. The coming into existence of the world was the outcome of a deliberate act of conscious, designful Will by a wholly transcendent, independent, and creatively active Agent, not a product of an undesigned, passive process—one in which the source is unaffected by its own effects, as is the case, for ex-

---

[24] Plotinus, *Enneads*, trans. Stephen Mackenna.

ample, with a shadow cast by an object, or the light or heat emanating from its source.[25] In further opposition to a Plotinian view, according to the terminology of the founders of orthodox Jewish and Christian theology, the world was not *generated out of the essence* of God, but was *created out of nothing* (*ex nihilo*). As we shall see later, however, there were certain defenders of deviant or unorthodox views both in Christian and Jewish theology—Scotus Erigena would be an example of the former, and adherents of Jewish kabbalah of the latter—according to whom the creation of the world is to be understood in such a way that *nihil*, the "nothing" out of which the world was created, belongs to the essence of God.

St. Thomas Aquinas's discussion of the concept of creation in relation to the use of the expression *ex nihilo* has a central, influential, and representative place in the history of orthodox treatments of that doctrine. It is linked with other discussions in both Jewish and Muslim theology, in particular with those of Saadia, Alfarabi, and Maimonides.[26] Let us consider the way St. Thomas formulates the matter.[27] In considering the question whether "to create is to make something from nothing," St. Thomas focuses on the objection that in using the prepositional expression *from* (*ex*), in the phrase *ex nihilo*, we seem to do violence to the meaning of that expression, for it "expresses the relation of some cause, and especially of the material cause; as when we say that a statue is made from brass. But *nothing* cannot be the matter of being, nor in any way its cause. Therefore to create is not to make something from nothing" (*Summa*, Q. 45, Obj. 3). To this objection, and in justification of the meaningful use of the expression *ex*

[25] On the question of whether emanation in Plotinus is to be understood in terms of "necessity" or some form of "voluntarism," see J. M. Rist, *Plotinus: The Road to Reality* (Cambridge, Eng.: Cambridge University Press, 1967), chap. 6.

[26] See H. A. Wolfson, "The Meaning of *Ex Nihilo* in the Church Fathers, Arabic and Hebrew Philosophy, and St. Thomas," in *Studies in the History of Philosophy and Religion*, vol. I (Cambridge, Mass.: Harvard University Press, 1973), 207–221.

[27] See Thomas Aquinas, *Summa Theologica*, Q. 45, 1.

nihilo, he replies by pointing out other uses of the preposition *ex* than the one made use of in the objection. One such alternative use of "from" (as already pointed out by Aristotle) is that of "after," and has to do with a question of order: "When anything is said to be made from nothing, the preposition *from* [*ex*] does not signify a material cause, but only an order; as when we say, *from morning comes midday*—i.e., *after* morning comes midday" (*Summa*, Q. 45, 1, Reply Obj. 3). Hence the expression "from nothing" should be understood as meaning "after nonexistence." However, the use of "after" in this context should not be taken as having a temporal significance, inasmuch as time was created along with the creation of the world. There is a further use of "from" that St. Thomas also appeals to in his reply to the original objection. He points out that in saying "it is made from nothing" one means "*it is not made from anything*; just as if we were to say, *He speaks of nothing*, because he does not speak of anything" (*Summa*, Q. 45, 1, Reply Obj. 3).

As we have seen in the foregoing glimpse of orthodox theology's view of the notion of creation *ex nihilo*, there were various metaphysical conceptions, even aside from purely atheistic or materialist ones, that were unacceptable despite their use of such notions as "a divine ground and source for the cosmos," "creation," and "nothing." These included Plato's conception of an uncreated, preexistent matter out of which the world was created by a Divine Craftsman, as well as the Plotinian (or, in general, neo-Platonist) conception of emanation of lower orders of being, including the material universe and man, from the One.

Within the broad framework of a theistic metaphysics, many different variations were developed over the course of centuries in the interpretation of such central concepts as those of "God," "creation," and "nothing." Among these variants were those associated with certain versions of mystical and negative theology. Without venturing to explore the many intricacies and byways of this rich vein of speculation, we shall nevertheless examine one central theme in this area: that of the Boundless. My use of the term "Boundless" is intended to collect and encompass a number of other expressions used in the type of creational metaphysics I wish to examine. In the kabbalah it bears the name "Ein-Sof"; for Meister Eckhart it is "Godhead"; for Scotus Erigena it is "God." As distinguished from orthodox conceptions of God, creation, and nothing, as previously discussed, those working within this tradition fall back on and adapt certain ideas found in the doctrines of neo-Platonist emanationism, and also, in some cases, on the views of the Gnostics.[28] The chief departure from orthodox views concerning God and creation *ex nihilo* is the claim that what is referred to as "nothing" is a "stage in the process of emanation from God," an "aeon," "the first of the *Sefiroth*," a "negative attribute" of the very essence of the Creator from which "derivative," "secondary," and "lower levels of reality" arose—for example, the physical universe, including all material creatures.

My purpose in rehearsing some examples of this conceptual scenario (an ingenious yet wholly speculative exercise in myth-making) is to suggest that the notion of "nothing," when disengaged and liberated from its association with a creational or emanationist metaphysics, provides an important and fruitful type of metaphysical insight. When so disengaged, "nothing" will be relabeled "Boundless Existence" in my own scheme of metaphysics, to be discussed later. However, in distinction from orthodox theology, whether creational or emanationist, I argue it is only *within* the observable universe—however our conception of the latter is enlarged by ongoing inquiry—where we should find examples of creation and causation. The latter concepts of creation and causation do not describe links *between* Boundless Existence and the observable universe.

A good place to begin, in reviewing earlier adumbrations of an acceptable notion of nothing, though still within the framework of traditional theistic metaphysics, is by considering the use of

[28] On gnosticism, see Hans Jonas, *The Gnostic Religion*, 2d ed. (Boston: Beacon Press, 1958).

the term "Ein-Sof" as introduced by the early kabbalists[29] of Provence and Spain in the late twelfth and early thirteenth centuries.[30]

The term "Ein-Sof" may be translated as "infinite" or "boundless." In Hebrew, the term would normally have been used in an adverbial way, meaning "extending without limit" when applied, for example, to describe God's existence and thought. The kabbalists transformed this adverbial expression into a proper noun and used it along with other expressions as a technical name for God.[31] The key idea conveyed by the use of this expression is that it has to do with the total absence of any distinctions and differentiations that, if present, might have allowed some form of comprehension and knowledge to be had of God. Insofar as God is referred to by this name, there is no claim that one may describe God as the First Cause, the Creator of the World, the Lawgiver, and so on. As Ein-Sof, God is not even "rationally inferred" or "revealed" through his creation. As Ein-Sof, God is totally con-

[29] The capitalized term "Kabbalah" designates an esoteric tradition or secret doctrine. Its contributors and adherents devoted much attention to the topic of Creation. The Hebrew term "bereshith" ("in the beginning . . .") with which the Book of Genesis opens, spawned a vast literature of commentary, commentary on commentaries, etc., known collectively as *bereshith* texts. Among these, *Yezirah* (*Book of Creation*) and the book *Bahir* played an important role and served in turn as starting points for numerous other works of interpretation.

[30] The pioneering scholarly works of Gershom Scholem are indispensable for a study of this field. See, for example, his *Origins of the Kabbalah*, ed. R.J.Z. Werblowsky, trans. A. Arkush (Princeton, N.J.: Princeton University Press, 1987); *Kabbalah* (Jerusalem: Keter Publishing House, 1974); *Major Trends in Jewish Mysticism* (London: Thames and Hudson, 1955).

[31] Scholem makes the following interesting remark concerning the Kabbalist penchant to regard all words as nouns: "It is, after all, one of the principles of mystical exegesis to interpret all words, if possible, as nouns. This emphasis on the noun character, on the name, may be taken as an indication of a more primitive attitude in the mystics' conception of language. In their view language is ultimately founded on a sequence of nouns that are nothing other than the names of the deity itself. In other words, language is itself a texture of mystical names" (*Origins of the Kabbalah*, 267). This view is clearly a close relative of the "Augustinian" approach to language we shall consider in chapter 3, in connection with Wittgenstein's critique of this dominant traditional view.

cealed, altogether beyond thought or the use of concepts of any sort, whether these concepts be borrowed from their use in connection with the domain of persons or of impersonal things. And this leads in one direction to identifying the Ein-Sof with nothing—in short, with the total absence of any distinctions or properties whatsoever.

At this point, in order to convey this aspect of Divinity, the kabbalists will typically emulate, in their own way, the use of the mythological terminology of "aeons" by the Gnostics or of "emanations" by neo-Platonists. In so doing, they will make use of their own myth-laden terminology concerning the ten Sefiroth that constitute the "emanations" within the life of the Divine. The kabbalists recognize a fundamental mystery, a total lack of any actual or possible explanation of what led God to "emerge" from concealment and manifest himself in creation. Scholem summarizes this doctrine as follows:

> The decision to emerge from concealment into manifestation and creation is not in any sense a process which is a necessary consequence of the essence of *Ein-Sof*; it is a free decision which remains a constant and impenetrable mystery. . . . These first outward steps, as a result of which Divinity becomes accessible to the contemplative probings of the kabbalist, take place within God Himself. . . . Here the Kabbalah departs from all rationalistic presentations of creation and assumes the character of a theosophic doctrine, that is, one concerned with the inner life and processes of God Himself.[32]

To convey this impenetrable mystery, and to describe this "inner process" in the Divine that "precedes" creation, some kabbalists use the concept of nothingness as the first "stage" or "Sefirah" in the emanative process. The term "Ayin" (absolute nothingness) will be used to symbolize the total barrier that separates the Hidden God both from other "later" stages of the "in-

[32] Scholem, *Kabbalah*, 91.

ner processes within the One," and from the creation itself, that is, all things that exist apart from God. According to Scholem, this marks a daring departure from orthodox theories of creation *ex nihilo*:

> Its particular importance is seen in the radical transformation of the doctrine of *creatio ex nihilo* into a mystical theory stating the precise opposite of what appears to be the literal meaning of the phrase. From this point of view it makes no difference whether *Ein-Sof* is the true *ayin* or whether this *ayin* is the first emanation of *Ein-Sof*. From either angle, the monotheistic theory of *creatio ex nihilo* loses its original meaning and is completely reversed by the esoteric content of the formula. Since the early kabbalists allowed no interruption of the stream of emanation from the first *Sefirah* to its consolidation in the worlds familiar to medieval cosmology, *creatio ex nihilo* may be interpreted as creation from within God Himself.[33]

Johannes Scotus Erigena, who lived in the ninth century and thus antedated the work of the Jewish kabbalists of France and Spain by four centuries, is a major metaphysician in the tradition of Christian mysticism who made important contributions to the concepts of creation and nothing. He made certain distinctions in connection with these that have strong affinities with those championed by the kabbalists.[34] Erigena, too, identifies *ex nihilo* with God's total unknowability, incomprehensibility, ineffability, and "nonexistence," and therefore with something that may be regarded as an "emanation" of God. In his major work, *On the Division of Nature*, Erigena makes a fundamental division in Nature—Erigena's name for "all things"—between those things that are (*ea quae sunt*) and those that are not (*ea quae non sunt*). By "things that are" is meant all that may be comprehended by sense

[33] Scholem, *Kabbalah*, 94.
[34] Henry Bett's *Johannes Scotus Erigena* (Cambridge, Eng.: Cambridge University Press, 1925; reprinted, New York: Russell and Russell, 1964) is a careful summary and exposition of Erigena's philosophy.

and intellect, whereas "things that are not" means all those things whose very *esse* surpasses sense and intellect, and so lack all comprehensible existence (*essentia*).[35] According to Erigena, we know that God exists, but not what God is. God does not have a comprehensible existence. And this, in one meaning of *nihil* or "nonexistence," is tantamount to saying that God is nonexistent.

This meaning of nonexistence goes back to a distinction made by Aristotle, who, in discussing "essential nonexistence" (as distinguished from "accidental nonexistence"), characterized nonexistence as "privation" (*steresis*). However, within privation Aristotle made a further distinction between that which has an absence of form[36] and that which involves "the forcible removal of anything."[37] When Erigena says of God that he has nonexistence, he means that God has essential nonexistence in the way Aristotle uses one meaning of privation to refer to absence of form.[38] In the traditional expression "creation *ex nihilo*," the term *nihil*, according to Erigena, is to be understood to signify "not merely the privation of habitude or the absence of existence, but the total negation of habitude, existence, substance, accidents, and of all that can be said or thought," and as such "it necessarily means God, Who is the negation of all that is, as being utterly beyond all that is."[39] This sense of "universal negation" applies to God, since only God cannot be spoken of or thought of. Therefore, in saying that the world was created from nothing, one is in effect saying that the nothing from which the world was created refers to God.

The following is an excellent summary of Erigena's main thesis:

> We may affirm the existence of God, and we may have a spiritual assurance of it, but we can no more define and ex-

---

[35] *De Divisione Naturae*, 643D (Bett, *Erigena*, 20). This and other references to this work are taken from Bett's summary and exposition.

[36] *Physics* I, 192a, 3–5.

[37] *Metaphysics* V, 27, 1022b, 31.

[38] Cf. H. A. Wolfson, *Studies in the History and Philosophy of Religion*, I, 205–206, 209–210.

[39] *De Div. Nat.*, 686; Bett, *Erigena*, 34; cf. Wolfson, *Studies*, I, 209–210.

press and comprehend His existence than we can the existence of nothingness. The terms *Deus* and *nihil* are therefore logically equal: both express something beyond the pale of existence *as we know it* in the universe. . . .

If we want to name some particular thing in a foreign language and we do not know the proper name of it in that language, we can only suggest what we mean in one of two ways. So far as our command of the language extends, we can say what the thing is like, or we can say what it is not. So it is in any doctrine of God: we are trying to name the Nameless. We may use the method of metaphor, and say what God is like,—Love, Light, the King of Kings, the Judge of all, the Heavenly Father,—or we may use the method of negation, and say what God is not—not local, not temporal, not limited in knowledge, not limited in power, not existing as any other being exists, not knowing as any other being knows. Now it is obvious that the first method is that of practical religion, and rightly so, for it is the most vivid and the most popular; but it is equally obvious that metaphor is out of place in metaphysics, and that if we are to make any philosophic statements about God at all, they must be negative in form, that they may suggest a limitless positivity for which we have no other language.[40]

Once we relinquish the reliance on misleading or unacceptable imagery and metaphors, is there anything that can be salvaged from the above account of theism's use of the concepts of creation and nothing? Can they be made to serve as helpful aids or clues in reaching our own answers to the question of reality? There is, and I would suggest that a first step is to drop the use of the word "God" and the theological use of "Creation." For the use of the first term imparts and retains misleading associations

---

[40] Bett, *Erigena*, 97, 99. For an interesting anticipation of some of Erigena's ideas as far back as pre-Socratic thought, particularly in the philosophy of Parmenides, see my *Cosmic Understanding*, 34–46, and "Making Sense of Parmenides" in my *Existence and Logic* (New York: New York University Press, 1974), chap. 2.

with the concept of a person, and the second imparts and retains misleading associations with the concepts of making and causal efficacy. In place of "God" I shall later (in chapter 4) introduce the capitalized expression "Reality." Furthermore, as my later discussion will undertake to show, we should do well to abstain from using the term "creation" altogether to describe the supposed "relation" between Boundless Existence and the observable universe, retaining the term "creation" instead under a restricted and limited sense as holding only *within* the domain of existents, that is to say, in connection with those parts of the observable universe (for example, human beings) that can be properly identified as creative agents. What about "nothing"? Here, I suggest, we may extract a very valuable insight from mystical theology as represented by the kabbalah and Scotus Erigena. Of course, before we can adapt these insights, we must be careful to rid ourselves of the myth-laden terminology of "emanations," "aeons," "Sefiroth," "barriers," and all the rest—which, if taken literally and not at best as exuberant exercises in symbolism and poetry, is notoriously the breeding ground of all sorts of nonsense. Once we understand the use of the term "nothing" in this context as signifying *total absence of form or intelligibility*, we should say Boundless Existence has no intelligible form or structure: it *is* nothing. In saying this, I should stress that I am *not* referring to the discoverable properties of the observable universe or any of its contents. For as contrasted with Boundless Existence, we *are* able to recognize, describe, and render intelligible all sorts of occurrences, phenomena, and objects within the observable universe.

TWO

The Kantian Revolution

Anyone dealing with the central metaphysical question of reality is confronted, sooner or later, by closely related philosophical questions concerning the analysis to be given to the central epistemological concepts of *knowledge* and *truth*. Since the major project of this book is to see how far we might venture in the direction of "answering" the question of reality by adopting as the basic framework in such an attempt the distinction between Boundless Existence and the observable universe, we shall want to explore the bearings of some core issues of epistemology on this distinction.

A good place to begin—because it provides some important, influential, and useful distinctions of its own—is by recalling some of the main contentions and innovative proposals of Immanuel Kant's critical philosophy. For in it, among other matters, Kant draws a fundamental contrast between the realm of appearances (phenomena) and a domain of cognitively inaccessible things-in-themselves (noumena). And this is a distinction that, with suitable clarifications and modifications, we may wish to adapt and apply in one direction in giving an account of the distinction between Boundless Existence and the observable universe. To benefit from Kant's discussion, we must try to understand, in the first place, what led him to draw his own distinction

65

between "appearance" and "reality," and secondly, what we can say for or against his way of justifying it.

The importance of examining epistemological questions was brought into prominence because of the kinds of emphases found in Descartes' system of thought. In that system, Descartes argued for the importance of beginning with the undoubted *existence of the individual human mind and its ideas* as a fundamental principle for all subsequent inquiries. Descartes selected the statement *"Cogito, ergo sum"* ("I think, therefore I am") as the axiomatic, unquestionable foundation for his own system of philosophy. It is the acceptance of this starting point that prompted Descartes, and those whom he influenced, to focus on the importance of raising questions about what lies "beyond" the mind and its ideas, particularly the extent to which these ideas can be relied on to provide reliable knowledge of the inherent properties and relations of objects in the external world. Such questions, and the many answers to them, belong to the philosophical discipline of epistemology.

We must of course remember that even though he started with the *cogito*, Descartes' principal motivation was to argue for the scientific goal of approaching the universe as a vast mechanism that can be understood by using the conceptual tools of the mathematical physicist. Yet Descartes was enough of a traditionalist to incorporate much of medieval theistic metaphysics in his system of thought—for example, the belief in the transcendence of God as a Creator, and in the existence of the human soul as an immaterial, spiritual substance joined to a mortal physical body. However, the fact remains that because Descartes assigned prominence to the *cogito* as the absolutely first principle of philosophy, from which even the existence of the soul-substance, God, and the physical world could be rationally derived, this shift in viewpoint spawned a whole new orientation toward philosophy. By drawing a fundamental distinction between the ideas that are "in" the mind and what is "outside" the mind (the "external world"), and by distinguishing the mind as a thinking spiritual substance in contrast to the physical substances of the external world, Descartes set up a framework that has had wide and deep repercussions in all of modern philosophy. We cannot understand the work of the British empiricists, the continental rationalists (for example, Spinoza), and the epoch-making work of Kant in the eighteenth century without remembering the fact that they all adopted, in one form or another, certain of the main presuppositions of Cartesian thought. Those presuppositions, particularly (1) the distinction between ideas "in" the mind and what exists "outside" the mind, and (2) the claim that the truth of ideas is to be judged in terms of how well they succeed in describing the external world, led to a detailed exploration of the distinction between "appearance and reality." The various schools of epistemological dualism (as in Locke), of subjective idealism (as in Berkeley), of philosophical skepticism (as in Hume), of solipsism, and Kant's distinction between the domain of mind-engendered phenomena and the domain of noumena are all offshoots of the Cartesian epistemological orientation to the problems of metaphysics.

Animated in part by the same goal as that of the logical positivists to "eliminate metaphysics," Kant anticipated some of their chief criticisms by carrying out his own type of assault in his major work, *Critique of Pure Reason* (1781, 1787). Indeed, when considered against the general background of the development of philosophy in the West, his attack proved to be far more subtle, elaborate, revolutionary in its implications, and long-lived in its repercussions.

In the *Critique*, Kant set himself a twofold task. On the one hand, he undertook to determine the general conditions under which human beings may be said to already have, or be hopeful of obtaining, genuine knowledge. Kant's answer to this question amounts to his analysis of the nature and scope of science, when this term is taken in its broadest sense. This account is given in the sections of the *Critique* called the "Transcendental Aesthetic" and "Transcendental Analytic." The former section deals with the question "how it is possible" for mathematics to offer such genuine knowledge—for example, in geometry and arithmetic.

The latter section gives Kant's detailed analysis of "how it is possible," that is to say, what are the necessary conditions for grounding the legitimate aspirations and achievements of the natural sciences.

A second major goal of the *Critique* was to show that the claim of certain types of traditional metaphysics to be able to provide genuine knowledge is misguided and bound to fail. For this purpose, Kant concentrated his attention on the conception of metaphysics exemplified in Christian Wolff.[1] This rested on an appeal to the methods of pure reason, unmixed with any appeal to sensible experience, to reach conclusions in rational theology, rational psychology, and rational cosmology concerning their respective subject matters: God, the soul, and the universe as a whole. Kant undertook to prove that there neither is nor could be any genuine knowledge concerning the latter topics, since they concern entities whose very existence and nature are entirely inaccessible to observational experience. Kant explores in detail the reasons for these kinds of failure in the section of the *Critique* called "Transcendental Dialectic."

According to Kant, science offers genuine knowledge because it stays within the bounds of a limiting but very general conceptual framework[2] that demands, for its proper use and application,

[1] Christian Wolff (1679–1754) was a leading academic representative of the German Enlightenment and a prolific author of textbooks in both German and Latin. He was much concerned to set out elaborate schemes for classifying the various branches of human knowledge. In this, he was strongly influenced by the orthodoxies of medieval scholasticism as well as by the main ideas of Leibnizian rationalism. For a brief account of Wolff's account of the scope and methods of metaphysics, see his *Preliminary Discourse on Philosophy in General* [1728], trans. R. C. Blackwell (New York: Bobbs-Merrill, 1963).

[2] I am here using the expression "limiting conceptual framework" in a very general way, to include what Kant would identify as Forms of Intuition (Space and Time) as well as the Categories and Principles of the Understanding. In the narrower use of the term "concepts," we should need not only to distinguish the use of concepts from the use of the Forms of Intuition, but also make a further distinction within the class of concepts between those that constitute the a priori categories of the understanding (and the principles of the understanding that explicate their meaning), on the one hand, and on the other, the empirical concepts

reference to what can be observationally experienced. On the other hand, the reason for the inevitable failure of metaphysics of the transcendent, nonempirical, purely rational variety is that it lies beyond all possibility of empirical determination. The attempt to offer *knowledge* of the soul, God, or the universe as a whole by making assertions about subject matters that could not be tested by observational experience must therefore be rejected and eliminated.

It is worth stressing, in the light of this brief summary, that Kant's principal target was the *transcendent metaphysics of pure reason*, not *all* conceptions of metaphysics. He had his own preferred conception of a sound and important form in which metaphysics *can* be retained. It goes by the name "transcendental philosophy": a metaphysics of experience. It offers a knowledge of the broad conceptual conditions that the human mind brings to bear in all inquiries of an empirical sort. This sense of "metaphysics" turns away from a pretension to set out the properties of a subject matter that exists altogether independently of human inquiry. It focuses, instead, on what the human mind brings to bear in any properly conducted empirical inquiry, the contribution it makes through its own cognitive apparatus. The metaphysics of experience is thus an inquiry of an epistemological sort, a "scientific metaphysics."

Insofar as Kant restricted himself to the twofold task of defining the scope of science and of rejecting the conception and practice of metaphysics as an attempt to obtain knowledge by means of pure reason of entities that transcend all possible observational experience, we could say his project is to replace a transcendent metaphysics of pure reason with a metaphysics of experience.

---

or empirical judgments that involve the application of the pure categories of the understanding to specific empirical materials and subject matters. For purposes of giving a rough and general account of how Kant wishes to characterize empirical knowledge, I am using the expression "limiting conceptual framework" in a way that does not draw the above distinctions—distinctions that would surely be needed in a more refined discussion of Kant's analysis of the structure of empirical knowledge.

However, if one were to ask Kant what he thought he had accomplished in setting out the limiting framework for all empirical knowledge, he would have said that he is offering a special type of knowledge: the discovery of certain necessary, "prewired" ordering conditions and rules of the mind's operation that are both synthetic (informative) and a priori. While not directed at such transcendent nonempirical entities as the soul, God, or the universe as a whole, the target of Kant's inquiry is still nonempirical. It is not found *through* experience. It is the purview of transcendental philosophy: a special form of metaphysics that Kant valued highly and claimed to have been the first to explore adequately.

At the heart of Kant's major innovative revolution in philosophy is the set of doctrines that go by the name of *transcendental idealism*. It was the discovery and articulation of the insights of transcendental idealism that Kant considered his chief accomplishments. For Kant, however, this form of idealist philosophy is to be sharply distinguished from, and is in direct opposition to any form of subjective, Berkeleyan, "problematic," "dogmatic," or "empirical" idealism. From Kant's point of view, the latter type of philosophy recognizes only the existence of minds and their "inner" subjective ideas, while denying the "objective" existence of material bodies in "external" space. His own philosophy of transcendental idealism, Kant insists, does not involve a denial of the real existence of material bodies in space. He calls the insistence on the reality of such material bodies in space "empirical realism," and maintains it is perfectly compatible with his own transcendental idealist views. However, it turns out that since, for Kant, space itself is a mind-imposed Form of Intuition used in ordering the unordered flux of sensory data, this type of "empirical realism" is only another part of the system of transcendental *idealist* metaphysics. Therefore, any evaluation of Kant's espousal of "empirical realism" ultimately depends on one's readiness to accept the central theses of transcendental idealism.

The way Kant formulates his central problem and gives his answer to it is so original, highly articulated, and impressive that it marks a watershed in the entire history of philosophy. We may call it the "Kantian revolution"; he called it his own form of "Copernican revolution." To put it briefly, what Kant set out to show in his own system of transcendental idealism (in opposition to the widely prevalent realist philosophy) is that if we are to understand in what genuine knowledge consists, we must pay crucial attention not simply to the traits of the subject matter we would describe or explain, but to the human conditions: the sensible ("aesthetic") and conceptual bounds that human beings impose on any subject matter. These bounds are already set prior to any investigation; they are not determined by the world independently of our investigation and to which we must accommodate ourselves, but consist rather in what we bring to bear in seeking knowledge and in setting out any results attained. The heart of Kant's critical philosophy is the claim that there are certain a priori, universal, and necessary conditions and rules for ordering experience that belong to the mind's cognitive constitution. These a priori conditions and rules for ordering experience are brought into play in the course of acquiring sound empirical knowledge. Kant undertook to show, therefore, that the dominant realist presuppositions, prevalent in the philosophies of his own day as well as in those of earlier periods, were in need of thorough critical examination and major overhaul. Rather than say with the traditional realist that, where there is knowledge, thought must *conform* to reality (that the achievement of knowledge is to be characterized simply as reaching true descriptive or explanatory judgments by virtue of being in conformity with the independent, inherent properties of objects), one should say, instead, that in cases of genuine knowledge there is an important sense in which *reality must conform to thought.*

We shall see, however, that even though Kant sought to challenge traditional realism because of its general failure to recognize the insights brought to light by his own transcendental philosophy, he did not entirely disassociate himself from all realist commitments. One aspect of his adherence to certain elements of traditional realism is his retention of the notion of the independently real existence of "things-in-themselves." In adhering to this attenuated and residual realism, Kant showed his refusal to accept the position of the skeptic who denies the very existence of "the external world."

How we judge the Kantian accomplishment turns on our evaluation of the philosophy of transcendental idealism. The effects of taking the point of view of Kant's transcendental idealism are still being felt. To properly digest and accommodate ourselves to the insights it makes possible and to the problems these insights bring with them is a major challenge that continues to confront philosophy into our own day. Different philosophers meet this challenge in different ways. In any case, the one thing that cannot be done is to ignore the Kantian revolution. From the time when Kant first propounded these ideas to the present day, many commentators and critics have disputed the value of these innovative ideas. Most would not deny that there is much of value to be found in Kant's work. However, there is disagreement about the nature of the salvageable elements that could be disengaged from the general scheme of transcendental idealism and made to stand on their own feet. For example, Peter Strawson, in his influential book, *The Bounds of Sense*, finds much of value in Kant's efforts to identify a basic set of conceptual means for organizing our perceptual experience. At the same time, he looks upon the whole scheme of transcendental idealism as philosophically "disastrous," since it rests on Kant's setting up a mythical conception of a cognitive apparatus that is modeled on, but not to be confused with, the structure of the empirically discoverable self. According to Strawson, this fateful but erroneous initial step led to Kant's own version of a transcendent metaphysics. Moreover, despite Kant's protestations to the contrary, Strawson sees Kant's scheme of transcendental idealism as having a closer affinity to a Berkeleyan type of subjective idealism and phenomenalism than Kant is able or willing to recognize, and therefore prevents it at bottom from being an acceptable or viable philosophy. In opposition to this and other deflationary treatments of Kant's espousal of the philosophy of transcendental idealism, other philosophic commentators, from Kant's day to our own, have taken a different, more favorable view of these doctrines. It is one of the purposes of my own investigation to show that the philosophy of transcendental idealism is not to be rejected as a mass of incoherences: that there are, on the contrary, important insights lodged in Kant's reorientation vis-à-vis traditional realist philosophies, but that these insights are obscured and rendered controversial by virtue of a number of features that, although Kant took them to be obvious or indispensable, are in fact obstructive to a sympathetic contemporary concern to uphold its main message and insights.

In carrying out his total project of defining the scope of science and of showing the futility of a transcendent metaphysics that rests on arguments of pure reason, Kant focused on a single major problem. It is to justify the claim that there exist certain indispensable cognitive conditions (a priori ways of structuring sensory experience in spatial and temporal ways, and various judgments and rules for conceptually ordering experience) that human beings bring to bear as a result of their own universally shared cognitive framework. This framework sets the bounds within which the pursuit of all genuine knowledge must be carried out, whether of a common sense variety or in any of the natural sciences. The operation and application of this cognitive framework determine what it means to have conceptualized experience (empirical knowledge) at all. To set out the nature of this limiting cognitive framework is the task of transcendental philosophy.

Kant wished to determine how far it would be *possible* for human beings to go in their pursuit of knowledge. He did not wish to deny that one can pursue empirical knowledge indefinitely into the future, and in this sense "*without* limits." However he insisted that the pursuit of such knowledge and any successes achieved must fall within actual limits or bounds consisting of the fixed, a priori cognitive framework defining the universal structure of the human mind. Without this fixed framework, there could not be any genuine empirical knowledge at *any* stage of inquiry, however far and without limits this may be carried into the future. For Kant, to isolate and characterize this fixed framework amounted to finding out the necessary ordering conditions and rules that are brought into play whenever we can be said to genuinely know something and not merely to think about, imagine, or believe on grounds of faith.

As an example of an item belonging to this fixed cognitive framework, let us consider what for Kant is a case of a synthetic a priori judgment, one that possesses necessary truth of a transcendental variety. It is the judgment that "Every event has a cause." This proposition is informative, since it adds to our knowledge and does not simply explicate by analysis what is already contained in the meaning or definition of a concept. Thus, according to Kant, no amount of analysis of the concept of *event* contains in its meaning the notion of *cause*. If we believe in the truth of the statement that every event must have a cause, its necessity is a priori (not based on experience), yet it is synthetic because it adds to our knowledge. The truth of this and other examples of synthetic a priori judgments could not be warranted by any ordinary appeal to evidence gathered from observational experience. For if it were, it would have to consist in the application of a broad conceptual framework that determines what, in advance of an actual inquiry, is to be understood as "empirical." To determine in what this consists is precisely what Kant wants to establish. If successful in isolating its features, these would be exemplified in any particular empirical inquiry. They could not be determined as the outcome of such an inquiry. For the latter would yield, at best, only probable or contingent truths. And if a proposition is only contingently true, it might be false. However, if a proposition might be false, it cannot be said to be necessarily true. One must look, therefore, elsewhere for the ground of its necessity. And this Kant found in the fixed cognitive structure of the human mind; it exists independently of, and transcendentally prior to, any appeal to experience.

In short, we could not be said to have the capacity for knowledge if we were unable to order sensory experiences in temporal or spatial ways (Kant calls these ways "Forms of Intuition"), or if we were unable to use and understand the nature of what it is to be a cause or what it is to be an object having properties (Kant gives the name "Concepts of the Understanding" to such concepts as those of causality and substance). To have these capacities is an indispensable requirement without which we cannot have "thought and experience." They define the universal and necessary basis for all human knowledge, for *all* conceptualized experience. They constitute the unique and inescapable framework within which every genuine example of knowledge is to be found as an instance of its application.

From among the several results Kant claims to have reached, there is in particular one theme of relevance to our present investigation that repays more careful probing. This is the distinction he draws between the realm of *appearance* and *things-in-themselves*. Having established the existence of a fixed, universal, a priori cognitive framework in the human mind, Kant draws the general consequence that, without relying on and employing this set of forms of sensible experience and antecedently fixed rules for ordering experience, we cannot have any genuine empirical knowledge of objects.

Does this amount to saying, for Kant, that in the absence of bringing to bear this fixed cognitive framework, objects are unknowable? Kant's answer, in a general way, is "yes." From his analysis of the limiting framework that belongs to the human mind, and through whose operation and application to the raw data of sensory experience all sound knowledge might be reached, Kant derives the general conclusion that the presence of those constraining conditions in certain respects *prevents* the mind from achieving knowledge of how things are "in-themselves." If one wishes to know the truth about objects as they exist wholly independently of and antecedently to human inquiry, this cannot be done: there is an impenetrable screen that hides such objects from discovery of truths about them. The unavoidable filter that the mind uses in ordering and interpreting the raw materials of sensory experience yields knowledge of objects as phenomena, as appearances, not as they are in-themselves. Kant states this result in the preface to the second edition of the *Critique*, and devotes an important section in the main body of the text ("The Ground of the Distinction of all Objects in general into Phenomena and Noumena"[3]) to elaborating this distinction. In the preface he writes:

> That space and time are only forms of sensible intuition, and so only conditions of the existence of things as appearances; that, moreover, we have no concepts of understanding, and consequently no elements for the knowledge of things, save in so far as intuition can be given corresponding to these concepts; and that we can therefore have no knowledge of any object as thing in itself, but only in so far as it is an object of sensible intuition, that is, an appearance—all this is proved in the analytical part of the Critique. . . . Though we cannot *know* these objects as things in themselves, we must yet be in position at least to *think* them as things in themselves; otherwise we should be landed in the absurd conclusion that there can be appearance without anything that appears. [B xxvi–xxvii]

However, what Kant means by asserting that things-in-themselves are unknowable, and his grounds for saying so, are not uniform. He has different ways of characterizing "unknowability." We can distinguish the following three directions of analysis:

1. In one, Kant adheres to the traditional theological and Platonic type of view according to which the world was created by a Divine Maker. It was endowed, at its Creation, with its own inherent properties. Even if human beings cannot know what those properties are, they are known in their full truth by their Creator. On this view, objects in the world remain unknowable *for human beings*. However, they are not in principle "absolutely unknowable," for they are knowable by their Maker. This is one sense of "unknowable" according to which Kant would maintain that independently existing things-in-themselves are unknowable. Nev-

---

[3] Book II, chap. 3, of the Transcendental Analytic.

ertheless, this sense of the unknowability of things-in-themselves does not occupy the forefront of Kant's transcendental concerns when his chief purpose is to champion and convince others of the fresh insights and discoveries of the critical philosophy.

At the heart of that philosophy, as previously stressed, is the recognition of the use by human beings, in *their* knowledge-pursuing activities, of certain mind-imposed universal, necessary ordering mechanisms, rules, and truths. Let us suppose that we were convinced by Kant that there are such ways of ordering experience. How does he interpret "unknowability" in the light of their operation? Here there is a certain ambivalence on Kant's own part: two directions in which he responds.

2. Insofar as we acknowledge the presence of these universal, necessary conditions for ordering experience, then in applying them—in requiring that confirmed empirical judgments conform not only to the requirements of the synthetic a priori conditions, but to the requirements of specific observational conditions, materials, and data—we do acquire genuine knowledge of objects: *we can say we have discovered* the properties belonging to those objects. From this way of looking at the matter, knowledge of the properties of things *is* attainable, *provided we stay within the bounds of the universal, necessary ordering devices brought into operation by the mind.* On this approach, the only ground for saying that objects are *unknowable* comes into view in response to the question, "What are objects like apart from the use of these universal necessary conditions, rules, and truths?" The answer would have to be, "We don't know, and cannot know." This is an answer that allows to humans the possibility of genuinely knowing objects, but only under certain bounds and limits. Anything outside of these bounds is, for human beings, unknowable. *What* things-in-themselves are, or *whether* there are any objects apart from those known by human beings in terms of their own cognitive apparatus, is for human beings unknowable.

3. There is, however, a third way in which Kant interprets "unknowability." To say that objects are unknowable is to deny that the very universal, necessary conditions for obtaining knowl-

edge prescribed by the cognitive equipment of the mind hold for things-in-themselves. This more stringent, exclusionary position denies that human organizational forms—for example, the forms of space and time and the principles of the understanding—can be said to apply, even in a restrictive way, to things-in-themselves. On this view, things-in-themselves are totally unknowable, even though Kant would wish to say they exist, in some way, independently.[4]

Let us sum up the main points of the foregoing account of Kant's epistemology. Like the opposite fixed ends resting on land to which the various cables of a bridge are attached, there are two fixed poles to which Kant, in his critical philosophy, adhered with virtually unwavering loyalty. One of these was his own form of residual, inherited, or common sense *realism*. Unlike God as the *intellectus archetypus*, human minds do not create the world in which they find themselves. Even when he was forced by his own philosophy of transcendental idealism severely to curtail what we could be said to know of the properties of the constituent objects or entities in the world created by God, and to resort to the notion of unknowable things-in-themselves, Kant did not cut his umbilical cord of his attachment to realism. He was not a pure subjective idealist or mentalist in his metaphysics. The other fixed pole of his philosophy was the conviction that the mind brings to its cognitive activities a set of antecedently present, necessary ordering devices, rules, and truths that belong to its own cognitive equipment and which it imposes on raw, unordered sensory "givens."

The major problem of an epistemological sort, and therefore of a fruitful "metaphysics of experience" or "transcendental philosophy," was, for Kant, one of objective validity. Call the ordering devices and patterns with which the human mind is equipped its *representations*. Call the independently existing entities, the

---

[4] For a full discussion of these ambivalences in Kant, see Paul Guyer, *Kant and the Claims of Knowledge* (Cambridge, Eng.: Cambridge University Press, 1987).

minimally presupposed realities in the world that the mind does not bring into existence and to which the mind addresses its *cognitive inquiries*, the *objects* in the world. Then, as Kant had already formulated the underlying epistemological problem as early as 1772 in a letter to his disciple Marcus Herz, he asked: "On what basis rests the relation to the object of that which, in ourselves, we call representation?" In connection with the concept of the unknowability of things-in-themselves, we have seen something of the variety of answers that Kant gave to this question.

THREE

Wittgenstein Carries
the Revolution Forward

A characteristic feature of much twentieth-century philosophy is the widespread attention given to the phenomenon of language as providing a major entry point for a consideration of many of the traditional problems of philosophy. Ever since the seventeenth century, Cartesian-inspired approaches have dominated the work of many philosophers engaged in these problems, but many contemporary philosophers have sought to free themselves from that Cartesian heritage with its emphasis on the epistemological examination of the individual mind's "subjective ideas" in relation to "the external world." In its place, we find in contemporary thought a growing and widespread emphasis on studying the workings of language in the manifold forms of social and institutional life. This involves examining in careful detail the diverse uses of language in science, literature, politics, religion, and everyday affairs, as well as in the various branches of philosophy itself—in logic, ethics, and metaphysics.

Especially in his later writings, Ludwig Wittgenstein was a leading champion of and contributor to this general shift toward a philosophic study of the nature of language. In his own distinctive approach, Wittgenstein followed a broad Kantian-type path of giving strong emphasis to the "necessary conditions" for all cognitive pursuits. For Wittgenstein, however, these conditions were not to be conceived, as they were in Kant's critical philosophy, as consisting of an elaborate, quasi-psychological, and transcendental apparatus, lodged in an innately given, permanent, unique, and universally shared structure of the human mind. Unlike Kant, Wittgenstein stressed the role of language as a public and social institution, pluralized into countless language games, grammatical rules, and forms of representation—all constructed by men and applied by them in the multifarious "forms of life" in which they are generated and embedded, and in which they are repeatedly applied.

In following this path, Wittgenstein's underlying, persistent interest was twofold. On the one hand, he was concerned to describe the logic or grammar of the manifold uses of language and, on the other, to call attention, through numerous examples, to various pathologic breakdowns in the thought of philosophers (and others) that can be traced to a general failure to understand the forms, interrelations, and limits in the diverse uses of language.

My present interest is not to survey the many facets of Wittgenstein's total contribution to this broad topic. It is, rather, to focus, first of all, on a central strand in this rich fabric that consists in Wittgenstein's insistence on the need to recognize the "grammar" of diverse "forms of representation," especially in his later writings. Later, I shall turn to another theme to which he also made important contributions: the analysis of what he calls "world pictures." In examining these two themes, I am interested to see how world pictures are related to grammatical rules, and to determine what light their combined use throws on the general project of metaphysics in undertaking to answer the question of reality.

GRAMMATICAL RULES

In turning to Wittgenstein's later views of the nature of language—work that in certain crucial respects marked a revolutionary departure from his earlier views, as set forth in his *Tractatus Logico-Philosophicus*—it is important first to consider the way those later views analyze the concept of *meaning* in connection with linguistic expressions. Many of the innovative, revolutionary features of Wittgenstein's philosophy of language, as presented particularly in his *Philosophical Investigations*,[1] were developed in opposition to what Wittgenstein labels "the Augustinian picture of the essence of language."[2] In Wittgenstein's opinion, this picture has been responsible for many examples of misguided thinking and the source of much intellectual confusion. His later writings were devoted to a prolonged, many-sided effort to expose the deficiencies of this deeply entrenched, influential tradition, and to point the way to a fresh and sounder way of thinking.

According to the Augustinian picture, the meaning of a word is typically taken to be the object (or entity) designated by the word. The paradigm for this way of conceiving of the essence of linguistic meaning can be found in examining the typical situations in which language is learned in early childhood. In these, one detects the omnipresent use of ostensive definitions as a way of teaching the meaning of an expression commonly assigned to a perceptually encountered object. At the very beginning of his *Philosophical Investigations*, Wittgenstein quotes a few sentences from Augustine's *Confessions* in which the author describes his experience as a child in coming to learn the use of language:

> When they (my elders) named some object, and accordingly moved towards something, I saw this and I grasped that the thing was called by the sound they uttered when they meant to point it out. Their intention was shown by their bodily movements, as it were the natural language of all peoples: the expression of the face, the play of the eyes, the move-

[1] *Philosophical Investigations*, trans. G.E.M. Anscombe (Oxford: Basil Blackwell, 1953).

[2] Cf. G. P. Baker and P.M.S. Hacker, *Wittgenstein: Understanding and Meaning*, vol. 1 (Chicago: University of Chicago Press, 1980), chap. 1. My own discussion of Wittgenstein is much indebted to this and other works of these authors.

ment of other parts of the body, and the tone of voice which expresses our state of mind in seeking, having, rejecting, or avoiding something. Thus, as I heard words repeatedly used in their proper places in various sentences, I gradually learnt to understand what objects they signified; and after I had trained my mouth to form these signs, I used them to express my own desires. [3]

In Wittgenstein's opinion, these sentences provide a brief picture of how the essence of language is conceived by that ancient thinker. [4] Indeed, they are also of great importance in serving as a miniature model—a germinal prototype—for what innumerable others down the centuries have employed in one or another fashion as their own paradigm in coming to understand the nature of language. In terms of the learning situation of a young child, Wittgenstein presumes Augustine had in mind the learning of words for ordinary perceptually (ostensively) encountered objects such as a chair, table, bread, or the proper names of individual persons. However, for those guided by this approach to linguistic meaning and the examples it starts from, it is assumed that the meanings assigned to types of words other than those that serve as names for ordinary perceived objects can also be modeled on this elementary, common case. These other words can also be regarded as names standing for entities, though the latter may be of wholly different types from the common perceptual objects, and the manner of coming to identify them may be wholly different from reliance on simple perception.

The main thrust of an Augustinian-oriented picture of the na-

---

[3] Augustine, *Confessions*, I, 8; see Wittgenstein, *Philosophical Grammar*, ed. Rush Rhees, trans. by Anthony Kenny (Oxford: Basil Blackwell, 1974), secs. 19, 20.

[4] However, Augustine himself has a more elaborate theory of language than Wittgenstein's quotation from the *Confessions* would suggest. Indeed, in his other writings, for example the *De Magistro* (*Concerning the Teacher*), he criticizes the simpler theory suggested in the quotation. For a brief discussion of these matters, see "Semantics, History of" by Norman Kretzmann in P. Edwards, ed., *Encyclopedia of Philosophy*, vol. 8, 366.

ture of language (the roots of which are discernible already in the few sentences quoted above) focuses on two main ideas: (1) that the meaning of all words consists in the objects or entities with which they are individually correlated and for which they stand; and (2) that a sentence is basically a combination of names that describes how the designated objects or entities are linked to one another.

There are many variations of and extensions to this basic, primitive model. Different philosophers or special philosophical traditions that share in a common indebtedness to the Augustinian paradigm do not agree with one another in detail with respect to how they work out their own version of the original model: each displays its own preferences and emphases. Thus with respect to the "objects" or "entities" taken as fundamental in particular ontologies with which words are correlated, some will identify them with concrete objects of a material, perceptible sort. Others, for example, Platonists, will recognize, in addition to concrete (perceptible) objects, a domain of "abstract objects" accessible only through intellectual or rational means. In some traditional versions of theism, not only are all of God's creatures regarded as particular objects, entities, or beings, but God himself is regarded as the supreme, uncreated being or entity. And for purposes of referring to any of these entities or beings, whether natural or supernatural, appropriate names are the preferred linguistic means.[5] Still other philosophers will assign spe-

---

[5] Cf. the following remark by Hans Blumenberg: "In the classical writings of the Jewish Cabala, the statement is continually repeated that 'the entire Tora is nothing but the great Name of God.' But these names are not only appellations, but also designations of the various ways in which God operates and is active. When he speaks, he acts, as the account of the Creation shows, and since he is not a demiurge his action consists exclusively in naming the effects that he wants to achieve. For the Cabala, again, that means that 'the language of God has, in fact, no grammar. It is composed entirely of names.'

"The demiurge of the Platonic myth must also speak one single time, at the critical juncture of his work—he must, very significantly, apply rhetoric in order, by persuasion, to bring the *Ananke* [necessity] that opposes the execution of the Ideas in the cosmos into cosmic obedience. Beyond that, the language of names

cial priorities to "mental entities" (ideas, experiences, impressions, thoughts), and so on. Some ontologies are severely and reductively monistic, admitting only one basic type of entity in their conception of the basic makeup of reality. Others, such as dualism and pluralism, choose some particular combination of different types of "real" objects or entities in setting out their more diversified metaphysical schemes. Despite these differences, all adhere to the Augustinian view that the meaning of every word, when thoroughly clarified, consists in the particular type of entity or object for which that word stands.

Another common feature of philosophies of language dominated by the Augustinian picture in its extended form, that is, aside from its emphasis on treating words as names for objects or entities, is the corollary emphasis on regarding sentences or propositions in their "basic, logical nature," to be the giving of descriptions of some situation or state of affairs. A sentence or proposition, in this broad sense, is regarded as a concatenation of names whose combination, if true, matches the way things are in reality—the facts of the matter.

One of the principal motives in the working out of Wittgenstein's later philosophy of language was to "demythologize" and uproot the foregoing, briefly sketched, traditional approach to language insofar as it gave special prominence to names as the paradigms of the use of word meanings, and to descriptions as the paradigms of combinations of words in sentences. A principal concern of Wittgenstein was to call attention to the manifold different uses of lingusitic expressions of all sorts. "Ostensive definitions" and "names for objects" lose their preeminence and pri-

---

here already—and momentously—has that of numbers and geometrical figures superimposed on it. The biblical Creation, on the other hand, is a command to come into existence and a naming as existing. . . . Thus one of the presuppositions of the biblical story of Paradise is that the Creation is accessible and familiar to man by virtue of the fact that he knows how to call the creatures by their names." See *Work on Myth*, trans. Robert M. Wallace (Cambridge, Mass.: The MIT Press, 1985), 37.

ority, as does a concentration on the role of sentences or propositions, in their "basic logical nature," as "descriptions."

For Wittgenstein, a preferred orientation to understanding the presence of meaning in connection with linguistic expressions is found by examining what is involved in the giving of various types of explanations of such meaning. He writes: "The meaning of a word is what is explained by the explanation of the meaning. I.e.: if you want to understand the use of the word 'meaning,' look for what are called 'explanations of meaning.' "[6]

The word "explanation" has various uses, and to understand the sense in which Wittgenstein uses it above, it is necessary to distinguish it from another prominent use with which it should not be confused. As normally employed in the context of science, or even as frequently employed in everyday situations, to explain something is to give an account of its causal conditions. To explain the occurrence of rainbows, or to explain why I cannot find my keys where I thought I left them, is to refer to specific antecedent conditions, the occurrence or presence of which, now recognized, contributes to solving our problem. In this sense, a causal explanation is an empirical matter and can be criticized or revised in the light of the facts brought to light in the course of continuing inquiry. It invites questions concerning the truth or falsity of the explanation offered. However, when Wittgenstein appeals to the notion of explanation in the context of exploring the notion of what it is to give the meaning of a linguistic expression, he is not interested in the theories offered in one or another empirical science that describe, for example, the historical, psychological, social, or physiological causal conditions that led to the introduction of various expressions. Rather, the sense of "explanation" to which he does appeal concerns those activities in which one is involved in making explicit, teaching, or appealing to *rules that, for some community, govern the correct use of some linguistic expression.* This type of explanation introduces what belongs to the domain of stipulation and convention. As made

[6] *Philosophical Investigations*, I, sec. 560.

explicit for purposes of teaching or clarification, *grammatical rules of use* are said to explain, in the relevant sense, the meaning of a linguistic expression: "An explanation of a sign can replace the sign itself. This gives an important insight into the nature of the explanation of signs, and brings out a contrast between the idea of this sort of explanation and that of causal explanation."[7]

There are many diverse ways of explaining the meaning, that is, the rules of use, of some word, phrase, or sentence. In the case of words, what is traditionally called "verbal definition" that specifies a list of "essential" characteristics—by giving, for example, genus and species—is only one type of rule. This classical view of definition (adopted by Plato and Aristotle), in setting up as its requirement for the analysis of the meaning of a concept the specification of its essence, is far too restrictive. It wholly ignores or undervalues the genuine adequacy of other types of explanation of meaning. For example, in a typical Socratic dialogue where one might want to define "justice," "courage," "friendship," "knowledge," "piety," and so on, Socrates refuses to accept someone's offer to give a list of examples of the use of the term. Only a statement in general terms of its essence will be considered. Wittgenstein comments:

> The idea that in order to get clear about the meaning of a general term one had to find the common element in all its applications, has shackled philosophical investigation; for it has not only led to no result, but also made the philosopher dismiss as irrelevant the concrete cases, which alone could have helped him to understand the usage of the general term. When Socrates asks the question, "what is knowledge?" he does not even regard it as a *preliminary* answer to enumerate cases of knowledge. [*Theaetetus*, 146D–7C].[8]

[7] *Philosophical Grammar*, sec. 59.

[8] Wittgenstein, *The Blue and Brown Books* (Oxford: Basil Blackwell, 1958), 19f. Cf. the following, from Wittgenstein's *Philosophical Grammar*, sec. 76: "If I try to make clear to someone by characteristic examples the use of a word like 'wish,' it is quite likely that the other will adduce as an objection to the examples

In learning the use of the term "circle," young children need not fail to understand it if they do not understand the geometer's definition of its essence, for they may be helped to gain such understanding by being given various examples. Again, to gain an understanding of what is meant by "a day of the week," it may be sufficient to enumerate the days. An *ostensive definition* (as distinguished from a *verbal definition*) that attaches a name to some observationally encountered object, person, situation, or event is also one among a wide variety of explanations of meaning that provides rules of use for a linguistic expression and contributes to an understanding of its meaning: thus in explaining the use of a particular proper name for a person or building, it may be sufficient to identify the individual visually by means of a pointing gesture. Among various types of rules, some operate by giving *samples* that serve as paradigms (e.g., in teaching the use of "red" or "B-flat"). Some rely on the use of illustrations (e.g., on the printed page of the "real" object). Also, as Wittgenstein shows, there are many terms of a "family resemblance" variety, such as "game," "a Churchillian manner," or "plant," that cannot be defined by giving the essence. Instead, one may choose some example as a paradigm and then point out varying amounts of resemblance, overlap, and difference for other examples that fall within the range of the term explained. In short, for some purposes and in some contexts, explanations other than the clas-

---

I offered another one that suggests a different type of use. My answer then is that the new example may be useful in discussion, but isn't an objection to my examples. For I didn't want to say that those examples gave the essence of what one calls 'wishing.' At most they present different essences which are all signified by this word because of certain inter-relationships. The error is to suppose that we wanted the examples to illustrate the essence of wishing, and that the counter examples showed that this essence hadn't yet been correctly grasped. That is, as if our aim were to give a theory of wishing, which would have to explain every single case of wishing.

"The use of the words 'proposition,' 'language,' etc. has the haziness of the normal use of concept-words in our language. To think this makes them unusable, or ill-adapted to their purpose would be like wanting to say 'the warmth this stove gives is no use, because you can't feel where it begins and where it ends.' "

sic insistence on a definition by essence are altogether satisfactory and useful.

In their diversity and interconnections, rules that explain the meaning of some linguistic expression belong to what Wittgenstein calls, in a broad use of this term, *grammar*. Grammatical rules comprise a collection of *forms of representation* that allows them to serve as *norms of representation*. While in some special and limited cases the grammar of an expression involves correlating a name with an object, it is by no means the case that such correlation of words with objects is the basis for giving meaning and establishing the grammatical rules of use for all types of linguistic expressions.

Any particular language-scheme can be learned through the use of various "language-games." People show their linguistic competence by being able successfully to apply their understanding to various examples. The purposes served by linguistic competence are greatly varied: describing, explaining causally, giving commands, making requests, play-acting, constructing proofs, giving sermons, telling stories, and so on. The forms of representation, network of concepts, and language-schemes devised by human beings are not only extremely varied, they also change over time. The amount and pace of change vary. Like cities, habitations, and social structures, some schemes (or parts thereof) may have long careers and be quite stable, while others are more fluid and undergo ready or frequent displacement.

One important feature of the Wittgensteinian approach is the thesis that all of the various types of grammatical rules, when considered as norms of representation, are free, unconstrained, conventionally agreed-on, publicly shared ways of endowing words or other types of linguistic expressions with their meaning. In this sense, grammatical rules are arbitrary and are not beholden to reality insofar as the latter obtains independently of language-rules. Grammatical rules do not disclose and conform to what is already "there" in reality.

Thus even where some sample of "red" (say a piece of cloth) is appealed to as a paradigm for explaining the meaning of "red," this sample is incorporated as a part of the linguistic rule, and in that role is not to be thought of as also described by the term "red." The linguistic rule is neither true nor false. Once learned, the term "red" can be applied for purposes of describing the color of various objects, scenes, or surfaces. And these description-sentences are open to appraisal as true or false. A factual judgment is not a grammatical rule: it rests, instead, on two primary grounds: (1) the arbitrary, conventionally adopted grammatical rules that assign their meaning to the expressions used in stating the judgment; and (2) the situation in reality that determines whether the statement is true or false.

In general, then, norms of representation should be seen for what they are: human creations or conventional constructs, not a means for discovering or mirroring a putatively inherent, independently existing, essential structure in the world. We cannot justify the choice of a norm of representation by saying that one *discovers* it to be valid or true. One can offer arguments *within* the conceptual scheme of a particular norm of representation, but one cannot step outside that conceptual scheme and give reasons or proofs that it is "correct," since there is nothing in reality, apart from the use of some particular norm of representation or network of such norms of representation, that offers a basis or foothold for upholding this claim. "The connection between 'language and reality' is made by definition of words, and these belong to grammar, so that language remains self-contained and autonomous."⁹ Nor, of course, can one give evidence or reasons for the "inadequacy" of some proposed grammar by stepping into some other grammar, some other norm or form of representation, since to do so would only yield, in turn, arguments and evidence given sense by the grammatical rules appropriate to and accepted in this other grammar. However, this other grammar—this other way of looking at things—is equally arbitrary. It too is a humanly constructed scheme of representation. There is, in

⁹ *Philosophical Grammar*, 55.

short, no independent arbiter to which we can appeal in judging the adequacy of a particular scheme of forms of representation.

A further argument, enforcing the same conclusion, is this. Any description of what one claims to find through observational experience, as expressed by means of an empirical judgment, can be true or false. However, one cannot appeal to an alleged reality to establish the "truth" of the language-scheme (grammar) one favors. For in this case the distinction between the sense of the language and its supposed truth or falsity is wiped out: sense becomes identical with truth. Thus, let us suppose we use the assumed sense of some language-scheme to describe the reality under examination to determine the truth *or* falsity of the language-scheme. Then, whereas an ordinary empirical judgment can retain its sense even when it is shown to be false, in the case of a language-scheme treated as if it were comparable to an empirical judgment, any supposed *falsification* would immediately destroy the *sense* of the "language." Hence the only way of retaining the language-scheme, despite this "empirical" test or "confrontation with reality," is to deny the possibility of its being false. And this shows that the adoption of a language-scheme, unlike the assertion of an empirical judgment that is genuinely either true or false, is a matter of convention or stipulation, and not something that can be established as true or false.[10]

In summary, the basic forms of representation of which the grammar of our language is constituted are arbitrary. The grammar we use is autonomous: it is not determined by appealing to reality. The forms of representation are not discovered by consulting some independent subject matter, nor sanctioned as "correct" or "true" because they correspond to, or are mirrored in putatively independent, existing facts. There are no "independently existing facts" to be consulted for this purpose, since to describe the "facts" already requires the antecedent availability and use of a humanly created language. Nor are there any "bare

[10] Cf. G. E. Moore, "Wittgenstein's Lectures in 1930–33," in *Philosophical Papers* (London: Allen and Unwin, 1959), 277–280.

facts" as such. If we are to describe the properties and forms of "facts," we need the language provided by some a priori, humanly constructed norms and forms of representation to do so. Moreover, there is no guarantee or warrant for saying that only one such conceptual scheme is uniquely and ideally suited to do so. For there is no way of showing that the supposed ontological counterpart of some particular grammar or language scheme already exists embodied in the world, awaiting discovery and some process of matching to determine whether it has been correctly formulated and articulated.

Wittgenstein sums the main points of the foregoing as follows:

> The thing that's so difficult to understand can be expressed like this. As *long as* we remain in the province of the true-false games a change in the grammar can only lead us from *one* such game to another, and never from something true to something false. On the other hand if we go outside the province of these games, we don't any longer call it 'language' and 'grammar', and once again we don't come into contradiction with reality.[11]

The foregoing features of meaning, especially the distinction between grammatical rules and factual judgments, are not only illustrated by examining the nature of *word*-meaning, but can be shown to be both relevant and important for other types of language use as well. For example, the explanation of the meaning of a sentence is also a matter of employing a number of devices to make clear the rules for the use of the sentence and its possible applications. One such device is to give a paraphrase, or to translate the sentence into another already familiar language. And of course here too it is necessary to distinguish between coming to understand the meaning of a sentence—the grammatical rules on which it rests—and the application of these rules.

All uses of language exhibit an underlying scheme of grammatical rules and norms of representation by which human be-

[11] *Philosophical Grammar*, sec. 68.

ings conceptualize their experience. In stressing this broadened conception of grammar and grammatical rules, Wittgenstein selected a number of special areas to which he devoted a good deal of his attention, and in which he sought to expose a host of confusions.

One such major area is mathematics.[12] Here he took an approach in basic opposition to the Platonist philosophy of many mathematicians. According to the latter, mathematics is a formal science par excellence engaged in discovering and setting out eternal truths about various mathematical entities and their interrelations with one another. According to Wittgenstein, however, there is no independent domain or objective reality of abstract mathematical objects to be explored and reported on in mathematical discoveries. When considered as a pure inquiry—that is, apart from the usefulness of actual *applications* of mathematical formulas or calculational devices to the concerns of engineers or to the subject matters and interests of physics, economics, and other empirical sciences—one must say that mathematics, in all its branches and subdisciplines, is an activity of *constructing* grammatical rules. Not only axioms, postulates, and definitions, but proofs of theorems erected on the basis of the foregoing that together comprise different types of calculi and deductive systems, belong to the creative exercise of *forming rules*. These rules, once adopted and approved, specify how certain linguistic expressions—technical symbols, equations, diagrams, chains of reasoning—are to be understood. As such, these rules are neither true nor false. They do not mark discoveries of putatively independent realities belonging to an eternal realm of intelligible Forms.

Another area of special interest to Wittgenstein was psychology. His interest in it, however, was not as an empirical science engaged in formulating and testing various explanatory theories,

---

[12] Cf. *Remarks on the Foundations of Mathematics*, ed. G. H. von Wright, R. Rhees, G.E.M. Anscombe, trans. G.E.M. Anscombe, rev. ed. (Oxford: Blackwell, 1970); *Wittgenstein's Lectures on the Foundations of Mathematics, Cambridge 1939*, ed. C. Diamond (Sussex, Eng.: Harvester Press, 1976).

but rather in its underlying conceptual structure, in the language schemes it exhibits and relies on in offering its descriptions and explanations of mental phenomena. To this end, he devoted considerable attention to the examination of such expressions as "understanding," "wishing," "intending," "expecting," "remembering," "perceiving," "sensing," "imagining," and "recognizing." He did so in order to expose a multitude of confusions that can be linked to the harmful influence of the conception of mind prevalent in the Cartesian tradition. [13]

In considering the interest of empirical sciences in explaining natural phenomena, Wittgenstein's views are also of help in understanding the nature of "theories" and "laws." Here, too, grammatical rules functioning as norms of representation are illustrated in an important way. This is particularly seen in the free, creative constructions of scientists when they operate on the level of *theory*. A theory provides the language used in specific hypotheses and empirically supported beliefs. Hypotheses and empirical judgments are *applications* of the language of some theory. These applications typically take the form of *predictions* of looked-for observable results of some inference or calculation, *descriptive reports* of particular observations and experiments, *generalizations* of observed regularities, or causal *explanations* of any of the foregoing. All such predictions, descriptions, generalizations, and explanations are couched, at bottom, in the distinctive language-scheme of a specific theory. At any given time, there may indeed be available a number of partially or completely incommensurable, rival theories for providing such applications. Once formulated by making use of one or another set of theoretical concepts and a particular theory's basic principles, the applications of the

---

[13] In addition to *Philosophical Investigations*, see L. Wittgenstein, *Remarks on the Philosophy of Psychology*, vol. I, ed. G.E.M. Anscombe and G. H. von Wright, trans. G.E.M. Anscombe (Chicago: University of Chicago Press, 1980); vol. II, ed. G. H. von Wright and Heikki Nyman, trans. C. G. Luckhardt and M.A.E. Aue (Chicago: University of Chicago Press, 1980); L. Wittgenstein, *Last Writings on the Philosophy of Psychology*, vol. I, ed. G. H. von Wright and Heikki Nyman, trans. C. G. Luckhardt and M.A.E. Aue (Chicago: University of Chicago Press, 1982).

theory's distinctive language for purposes of description, prediction, lawlike generalization, or explanation are treated as empirical judgments. Insofar as the theory is evaluated as "true" or "false," this takes place on another level and in another sense from that in which a particular empirical judgment is so judged. The truth or falsity of an empirical judgment is determined directly by confrontation with the data of observation. In the case of a theory, on the other hand, it is more appropriate to use pragmatic criteria in judging the relative success in relying on its own grammar for formulating empirical judgments, as compared to the use of other theories. As contrasted with the way in which the adequacy of an empirical judgment is determined—by confrontation with observational materials—the adequacy of a theory is to be judged by taking into account the number and degree of instances of evidential support for the empirical judgments encompassed by the theory, as well as by its logical simplicity and elegance.

We come, finally, to philosophy itself. In his later writings, particularly in *Philosophical Investigations*, Wittgenstein calls attention to the underlying reasons for the chronic, irresolvable controversies found in much traditional philosophy, and he proposes how philosophy should be practiced in a genuinely constructive and fruitful way. The main task of philosophy, according to Wittgenstein, is to attain a *perspicuous representation*. He writes:

> A main source of our failure to understand is that we do not *command a clear view* of the use of our words.—Our grammar is lacking in this sort of perspicuity. A perspicuous representation produces just that understanding which consists in 'seeing connexions'. Hence the importance of finding and inventing *intermediate cases*.
>
> The concept of a perspicuous representation is of fundamental significance for us. It earmarks the form of account we give, the way we look at things. [14]

[14] *Philosophical Investigations*, I, sec. 122.

He describes this as consisting in a clear understanding of the grammar of our language. In saying this, the term "grammar" can be used in two ways.[15] On the one hand, philosophy as grammar stands for the *study or survey* yielding (when successful) a perspicuous representation. In another sense, the term "grammar" stands for the *subject matter* consisting of various norms of representation, conceptual interconnections, and grammatical rules studied by grammar in the first sense. The subject matter studied are norms of representation, "ways of looking at things." As such, norms of representation are neither true nor false; they consist of *linguistic conventions*. A careful grammatical survey— "a clear view of the use of our words"—not only gives the understanding or perspicuous representation that philosophy seeks, it also helps to achieve the therapeutic benefits of removing confusions and (dis)solving pseudo-problems. To accomplish these results, philosophy compares and contrasts various uses of language in different domains; it notes similarities and differences in uses; it exposes fallacies and intellectual confusions; it shows the reasons for getting entangled in "insoluble (intellectual) knots." In his own diagnoses of the focal causes of such pathology, Wittgenstein calls attention to the frequently harmful influence of patterns of thought belonging to the Platonist, Augustinian, or Cartesian traditions.

In particular, Wittgenstein makes many critical remarks intended to expose the futility of much metaphysical writing devoted to the attempt to discover and report the truth about the nature of reality. The traditional goal of metaphysics is frequently described as consisting in the desire to discover and articulate the *essence of reality*. Wittgenstein's thesis is that metaphysical statements that purport to offer such factual knowledge about the world are, at best, disguised a priori grammatical sentences and therefore are not to be judged as either true or false. Metaphysics "obliterates the distinction between factual and conceptual inves-

---

[15] Cf. P.M.S. Hacker, *Insight and Illusion* (Oxford: Clarendon Press, 1972), 150ff.

tigations."[16] In this respect, the ambition of traditional metaphysics is misguided, since talk about essence at best holds for conceptual connections, and is therefore a matter only of what the linguistic conventions, the grammar of our forms of representation, require and state. For Wittgenstein, essence belongs to the domain of grammar, not ontology. "*Essence* is expressed by grammar.[17] . . . It is not the property of an object that is ever 'essential', but rather the mark of a concept.[18] . . . If you talk about *essence*—, you are merely noting a convention. . . . To the *depth* that we see in the essence there corresponds the *deep* need for the convention."[19]

Hence, wherever we find a metaphysician declaring he has succeeded in uncovering and conveying the essence of the world, we can be sure that he is suffering from a pathological illusion endemic to all such forms of inquiry and speculation. This consists in taking as real what is at best only the projection onto reality of the system of concepts, of grammatical connections, stipulations, and conventions of a network of forms of representation. To overcome this illusion, we must rid ourselves of the belief that any grammar corresponds to an essential structure inherent in the world, that there is a unique and absolute truth of a metaphysical sort awaiting discovery by human beings.

A crucial feature that differentiates contemporary analytic philosophy from Kant's critical philosophy is the way in which synthetic a priori propositions are regarded. For Kant, such propositions are the embodiment of necessary truths. They are to be found in stating the distinctive contents and character of the Principles of the Understanding. In composing part of the fixed and universal cognitive structure and apparatus of the human mind, they are inevitably brought into play in all cases of genuine empirical knowledge. For philosophies such as Logical Positivism

---

[16] Wittgenstein, *Zettel*, ed. G.E.M. Anscombe, G. H. von Wright, trans. G.E.M. Anscombe (Oxford: Basil Blackwell, 1967), sec. 458.

[17] *Philosophical Investigations*, sec. 371.

[18] Wittgenstein, *Remarks on the Foundations of Mathematics*, I, sec. 73.

[19] *Remarks*, I, sec. 74.

and the later writings of Wittgenstein, no accreditation can be given to the very existence of genuine synthetic a priori propositions. They are a philosophic concoction, a pseudo-category—as are the philosophic problems that emerge from accepting their existence and finding ways of accommodating various other conceptions or beliefs to that acceptance. Indeed, many analytic philosophers will even abandon the very distinctions made prominent by Kant between "analytic" and "synthetic," as well as the classfication of judgments based on their use.

Wittgenstein's later writings in particular show a marked deviation from Kant's philosophic adherence to the notion of necessary truths that allegedly convey a species of metaphysical knowledge. Yet Wittgenstein's treatments of the notion of "necessity" also display a number of unmistakable family resemblances with the kinds of questions with which Kant was preoccupied. This concerns the kind of necessity that belongs to grammatical rules.

A central feature of Kant's epistemology or "metaphysics of experience" is its emphasis on the notion of necessity. This term, however, can be used in two different though related ways. In one direction, the term "necessary" or "necessity" is used in conjunction with the concept of *conditions*; in another direction, it is used in connection with *propositions*. With respect to conditions, one can make a distinction between *necessary conditions* and *sufficient conditions*. In the case of propositions, one can make a distinction between *necessary propositions* (or *propositions that are necessarily true, necessary truths*) and *contingent propositions* (or *propositions whose truth is contingent, contingent truths*).

With respect to conditions, let us distinguish two items, X and Y. Then to say X is a necessary condition for Y is equivalent to saying that unless X were present, Y would not occur or hold. For example, a necessary condition for being eligible to become president of the United States is being a citizen of the country. By contrast, where X is a sufficient condition for Y, it is one among a plurality of conditions such that Y could occur or hold in the presence of any one of that plurality. For example, a sufficient condition for being a candidate for a certain job might be having ten years of work experience, and another might be to have a college degree.

As used to mark a type of proposition, "necessity" refers to the fact that the truth of the proposition is regarded as being logically certain and unrevisable. On the other hand, a contingent proposition is one the acceptance of whose truth is provisional, since it is open to modification or abandonment.

One way in which these two different uses of "necessity" are joined is to specify of certain *necessary propositions* (*necessary truths*) as the X's that are *necessary conditions* for some Y. This is the situation in Kant's epistemology. He wishes to show that one type of necessary condition for defining genuine knowledge or for the realization of such knowledge is the presence, on a conceptual level, of certain necessary propositions conveying necessary truths.

One way of stating wherein Wittgenstein's philosophy deviates from Kant's is to focus on the notion of "necessity." As does Kant, Wittgenstein recognizes the importance of specifying certain necessary conditions that make possible the distinctive human capacities and activities devoted to the achievement of knowledge. However, Wittgenstein rejects Kant's claim that there are certain necessary truths we must include among the necessary conditions for achieving knowledge. In the phrase "necessary truths," accordingly, Wittgenstein would eliminate the term "truth" and retain the term "necessary" when discussing necessary conditions for the achievement of knowledge.

The use of language is among the necessary conditions for the achievement of knowledge. And one aspect of the use of language that contains, in turn, a specific type of necessary condition for the achievement of knowledge is the presence of grammatical rules. The latter specify or explain the meaning of various linguistic expressions. Grammatical rules have their own distinctive type of necessity, but it is not one of truth.[20]

[20] For a full discussion of this theme, see G. P. Baker and P.M.S. Hacker, *Wittgenstein: Rules, Grammar, and Necessity* (Oxford: Basil Blackwell, 1985).

Along with many others in the history of philosophy, Kant subscribed to the view that one class of necessary truths is to be found in the discipline of Formal Logic. They are usually formulated as, and considered to be, the Laws of Logic. Another class of necessary truths that Kant recognized is that which belongs to mathematics: these are found, according to traditional classifications, in arithmetic and geometry. In addition to the foregoing, Kant claimed there is an important set of necessary truths that his own explorations of Transcendental Logic (his "metaphysics of experience") isolated and established by various arguments. A distinctive problem that Kant's transcendental philosophy faced is that of accounting for the necessary truths he claims to find in mathematics and in empirical science. Kant's general answer to this question is that they belong to the permanent, fixed, and universally shared cognitive structure of the human mind. The human mind depends on the operation of these necessary truths. Where we have empirical knowledge, it is through the application of these necessary truths (these examples of metaphysical or transcendental knowledge) to the various materials furnished by sensory or perceptual experience.

One way of stating the fundamental difference between Wittgenstein and Kant is the following. According to Wittgenstein, where someone claims to display a necessary truth—for example, in logic, metaphysics, or mathematics—that person has only stated what is at bottom a grammatical rule, a convention, decision, or stipulation about the meaning to be given to some linguistic expression, say a word, sentence, or proof. Necessity is to be found only in the form of linguistic rules that stipulate or establish how certain expressions are to be understood. "Whenever we say that something *must* be the case we have given an indication of a rule for the regulation of our expression."[21] For ex-

---

[21] A. Ambrose, ed., *Wittgenstein's Lectures, Cambridge 1932-35* (Oxford: Basil Blackwell, 1979), 16. Further, Wittgenstein points out: "The statement that there must be a cause shows that we have got a rule of language. Whether all velocities can be accounted for by the assumption of invisible masses is a question of mathematics, or grammar, and is not to be settled by experience. It is settled before-

ample, where Kant thought the proposition "Every event has a cause" states a necessary truth (an item of transcendental knowledge, a description of an abiding state of affairs), Wittgenstein would say this proposition expresses a grammatical rule, a norm of representation, a stipulation about how to connect the concepts "event" and "cause." Similarly, propositions of mathematics do not state eternal truths. They offer a set of syntactical rules concerning such concepts as curvature, prime numbers, irrational numbers, and a host of others. For example, the axioms and theorems of Euclidean or non-Euclidean geometry specify rules for connecting the concepts they employ, such as "triangle" and "angle sum." If, for example, these concepts are used in formulating empirical propositions about the outcome of a land survey or in describing spatial relationships among astronomical objects, the meaning of those propositions is based, at least in part, on the grammatical rules of the particular geometry that has been applied. Hence, the problem that Kant thought calls for a solution, namely that of finding the justification for accepting certain propositions as stating necessary truths (as providing a certain kind of knowledge), does not arise. If there are no necessary truths, there is nothing to explain.

Grammatical rules, though they convey a type of necessity, are

---

hand. It is a question of the adopted norm of explanation. In a system of mechanics, for example, there is a system of causes, although there may be no causes in another system. A system could be made up in which we would use the expression 'My breakdown had no causes.' If we weighed a body on a balance and took the different readings several times over, we could either say that there is no such thing as absolutely accurate weighing *or* that each weighing is accurate but that the weight changes in an unaccountable manner. If we say we are not going to account for the changes, then we would have a system in which there are no causes. We ought not to say that there are no causes in nature, but only that we have a system in which there are no causes. Determinism and indeterminism are properties of a system which are fixed arbitrarily" (ibid, 16). These remarks have a clear bearing on current discussions of the question of determinism raised by quantum mechanics, and also on the analysis and evaluation of the scientific use of concepts of "chaos," "nonlinearity," and related topics currently much discussed.

not themselves true or false. It is even misleading to say they are "true by convention," as distinguished from being factually or empirically true. It is best to avoid the use of the terms "truth" or "true" altogether in considering the status of grammatical rules. If one does nevertheless continue to use these terms (and one could not consistently legislate them out of existence), it is important to distinguish their use in connection with grammatical rules from their use in connection with empirical propositions. Grammar is antecedent to factual or empirical truth, since it determines only conceptual connections; it is not itself a source of factual truth or a way of stating such a truth. Of an empirical proposition, since it can be true or false, we can say what would render it false. In the case of a norm of representation, however, it makes no sense to conceive what would be the case if it were false. For the alternative to one norm of representation thought to be "false" is not some other norm that is thought to be "true." It is only some other rule, convention, or way of formulating conceptual connections that is different.

Hence, if one is to explain or account for the existence or recognition of "necessary propositions," one should look elsewhere than for the kind of grounds to which traditional philosophers like Kant, Plato, or a host of others have looked. Kant supported his philosophy of transcendental idealism by exploring what he took to be the fixed, necessary structure of the human mind, the faculties or powers by which it approaches and interprets reality. In setting out the details of this structure, Kant showed himself to be strongly influenced by the underlying, background Cartesian conception of the mind as a subjective locus of "ideas" of various sorts contained "within" it, as contrasted with an "outer," "objective" world or reality. Kant never shed some aspects of this Cartesian orientation.

In contrast with the Cartesian approach to the mind with its distinction between "internal ideas" and an "external world," Wittgenstein concentrates on the fact of the construction, adoption, and use of various *public* grammatical rules that determine the sense of linguistic expressions. Unlike Kant's efforts to locate necessary truths, whose existence and exercise he was concerned to justify, by assigning them to the innate, fixed structure of the mind, Wittgenstein claims that the grammatical rules human beings construct, accept, and use are located in the public arena. They inform the practices of human communities and are shared by individuals who learn and accept already well-established rules, and in some cases, change or affect them by making original contributions to the common fund. But no single mind owns them. They are embedded in various forms of life, in the varied activities in which language performs its manifold uses, and not in the publicly inaccessible domain of someone's private mental experience. Moreover, like all social, cultural, and communal institutions, achievements, and practices, they are multiple, varied, and open to change. Like in cities, some features may persist and abide, others may undergo radical change or disappear altogether. In short, the rules that govern the meanings of our language are not fixed, unique, and universal. Their necessity is not fact stating or synthetic. As rules for forming conceptual representations, their necessity consists only in specifying and establishing conceptual connections. Their necessity arises from their being arbitrary stipulations and conventions that communities of people adopt. Hence their "relation" to objects is simply the application of these meaning-rules in various ways, including the formulation of empirical propositions.

Nor is there any question of finding out through experience whether the world sanctions or contains in its own putative inner structure a ground of agreement or disagreement with rules of grammar. The search for an answer to this question is fruitless, not because it is difficult to find or establish an answer, but because the question is incoherent and confused. As we saw at the end of chapter 2 in the quotation from Kant's letter to Marcus Herz, a major problem was to answer the question "on what basis rests the relation to the object of that which, in ourselves, we call representation." For Wittgenstein, there is no such problem of finding the "basis for the relation between representation and object." The necessity that characterizes a grammatical rule or any set of stipulations as to the bounds of sense (the scheme of representations used), however relatively simple or complicated, is an *internal necessity*. It establishes conceptual links among linguistic expressions (words, sentences, premises and conclusions in a mathematical proof, and so forth). There is no external necessity that binds a particular grammar or scheme of conceptual connections to reality. No one scheme can be "discovered" as the true one. To think there is a true scheme is a misleading myth shared by many philosophic systems. Choice among sets of rules is not settled by finding which of the available necessary propositions matches the putatively real, genuine, objective "facts." For there are no "objective facts of the matter."

The basis for choice from among available necessary propositions is, at bottom, a pragmatic one: how well an adopted set of rules works in practice. The use of the term "pragmatic" here is not intended to refer to a pragmatic theory of the *truth* of necessary propositions, as distinguished from other theories of what constitutes the truth for such propositions, since necessary propositions are not, as grammatical rules, to be considered as possessing any truth at all. Rather, the term "pragmatic" applies to the way of assessing the application of such rules in the course of offering various empirical propositions as true descriptions, explanations, or predictions of matters of fact. Thus Riemannian geometry is not truer than Euclidean geometry, nor vice versa, since neither is true. Each, however, offers, for example, its own rules for connecting the use of the terms "triangle" and "angle sum." For Riemannian geometry, the angle sum of a triangle is larger than 180 degrees by an amount that varies with the area of the triangle. In describing the angle sum of a very large triangle on the surface of the Earth, it would be more convenient to use the grammatical rules of Riemannian geometry than the grammatical rules of plane Euclidean geometry.

To summarize: In opposition to a thinker such as Kant who subscribed to the view that there are certain propositions that convey necessary truths as parts of the universal and fixed cognitive structure of the human mind, Wittgenstein denies there are such necessary truths. Instead, all alleged instances of necessary truths are only instances of grammatical rules. They are stipulations for giving meaning to certain expressions; they establish conceptual connections. But in so doing, they do not settle anything about what is true of reality. For that, one has to apply the grammatical rules to particular situations and use whatever criteria are considered appropriate in particular circumstances for determining what is true.

Suppose one were to ask, "But what, apart from the use of *any* grammar, any set of meaning-rules, is the nature of reality, of things-in-themselves?" The reply to this should be that this question cannot be answered, for the very attempt to answer it already violates the conditions being excluded by the question, namely to say what "things-in-themselves" are without using language. And this cannot be done because the request is self-contradictory. What reality is "in itself" is unsayable. But if one uses some grammar or other, it is possible to find out what is the case, what are the facts. However, there is no constraint or mustness that attaches to any one set of grammatical rules. There are multiple schemes available, and preferences are guided by habit, social inertia, or pragmatic considerations.

There is a fundamental contrast, in short, between Kant's and Wittgenstein's general response to the question, "What is the truth about reality?" For Kant, there is a domain of things-in-themselves; a knowledge of their properties is blocked by the interposition of the necessary truths in the mind's fixed structure. The operation of the latter yields only a realm of appearances, a phenomenal world, not reality as it is in itself. On a Wittgensteinian approach, we cannot say what reality is in itself apart from or independently of the use of any grammatical scheme, not because we are blocked from knowing it, but because the situation being envisaged is not possible. The question is incoherent and falls apart. However, this does not mean that there is no reality other than grammar. Wittgenstein's position is not one of "linguistic idealism." It is not the case that all that exists are grammatical rules! To determine what is true of reality one must first settle on some grammar that provides meaning-rules, and secondly, one must apply some set of criteria and procedures that specify in what truth about reality consists.

WORLD PICTURES

In his defense of the philosophy of Common Sense, British philosopher G. E. Moore (1873–1958) claimed certainty and unshakable knowledge for the truth of such propositions as that there are material objects in the universe, that he and other human beings have bodies, experience various conscious acts, hold beliefs of various sorts, and that the Earth existed before he was born.[22] Moore undertook to prove that these and many other propositions of Common Sense can be defended against philosophers who would deny them, and in particular against the views of a skeptic who would question the very existence of the external world. In championing his Common Sense philosophy, Moore accordingly devoted much attention to the use of such expressions as "I am certain," "I cannot be mistaken," and "I know."

In notes written toward the very end of his life and published posthumously as a book bearing the title *On Certainty*,[23] Wittgenstein critically examined these views of Moore and found various weaknesses in them. His motive was not to come to the aid of the skeptic or other metaphysicians who challenged the beliefs of Common Sense, but to show that Moore had misconstrued the use of such expressions as "I know," "I cannot be mistaken," or "I am certain." According to Wittgenstein, Moore had failed to draw certain important distinctions in their use, depending on whether the statements to which they are attached do or do not belong to a *world picture* (*Weltbild*). For "certainty," "knowledge," and similar terms of epistemological appraisal have an al-

[22] See G. E. Moore, "A Defence of Common Sense," in his *Philosophical Papers* (London: Allen and Unwin, 1959), 32–59, and his *Some Main Problems of Philosophy* (London: Allen and Unwin, 1953), 1–27.

[23] Ludwig Wittgenstein, *On Certainty*, ed. G.E.M. Anscombe and G. H. von Wright, trans. D. Paul and G.E.M. Anscombe (Oxford: Basil Blackwell, 1969).

together different use when applied to the beliefs that make up a person's world picture, as distinguished from their use in connection with the more fluid, variable set of beliefs that are not constitutive parts of a world picture. Wittgenstein proposed to classify the type of judgments Moore claimed to know, and concerning which Moore thought he could not be mistaken, as belonging to what Wittgenstein calls the *groundless* character of a world picture. As such, these judgments should not be confused with the cognitive status of other propositions, beliefs, or judgments for which it *is* relevant to inquire into their grounds.

In investigating the question of reality—and, in connection with this, the distinction between appearance and reality—it will be interesting to see the bearing of Wittgenstein's discusssion of world pictures on these issues.

When people claim to *know* that something is the case, it is normally accepted as relevant to ask for the grounds for their claim and for evidence to back it up. It is not an adequate reply for a person simply to express a feeling of certainty and to display an attitude of strong conviction. One looks for good reasons to support the claim to know such-and-such. In examining these reasons, it is helpful to distinguish between the method employed in supporting the claim, and the evidence appealed to. By "method" is meant *how* the person warrants or justifies the claim to know something—for example, by appealing to authority, experience, calculation, and so on. One type of "good reasons" concerns the adequacy or reliability of the method being used to support a claim to knowledge. Another way by which one looks for "good reasons" has to do with the evidence for the proposition. Let the expression "grounds in support of a claim to knowledge" be understood as covering both the methods used for justifying the claim as well as the specific evidence introduced in its behalf. The main point that Wittgenstein would make in connection with examining claims to knowledge is that such claims, when fully explored, are found to have a terminal, *groundless* base. The search for grounds comes to an end. If probed deeply enough, the justification of a claim to knowledge reveals an unquestioning reliance on *this* method and *these* pieces of evidence. "Justification by experience comes to an end. If it did not it would not be justification."[24] Similarly, the chain of evidence also must come to an end, if one is not to face the futile prospect of an infinite regress. In short, at the end of a process of unearthing grounds there is the *groundless*.

This terminus is what Wittgenstein calls a "world picture." In it, one encounters commitments or judgments that rebuff requests for *their* grounds. It consists of a network, framework, or system of concepts, beliefs, and practices that—for a person or group holding the world picture—is fixed, accepted, and unquestioned. Itself ungrounded, a world picture provides grounds for those practices, beliefs, judgments, inquiries, and projects that are fluid or open to test.

> Giving grounds, . . . justifying the evidence comes to an end. . . .[25] At the foundation of well-founded belief lies belief that is not founded.[26]
>
> Is it wrong for me to be guided in my actions by the propositions of physics? Am I to say I have no good ground for doing so? Isn't precisely this what we call a 'good ground'?
>
> Supposing we met people who did not regard that as a telling reason. Now, how do we imagine this? Instead of the physicist, they consult an oracle. (And for that we consider them primitive.) Is it wrong for them to consult an oracle and be guided by it?—If we call this "wrong" aren't we using our language-game as a base from which to *combat* theirs?
>
> And are we right or wrong to combat it? Of course there are all sorts of slogans which will be used to support our proceedings.
>
> Where two principles really do meet which cannot be reconciled with one another, then each man declares the other a fool and heretic.

[24] *Philosophical Investigations*, I, sec. 485.
[25] *On Certainty*, sec. 204.
[26] *On Certainty*, sec. 253.

I said I would 'combat' the other man,—but wouldn't I give him *reasons*? Certainly; but how far do they go? At the end of reasons comes *persuasion*. (Think what happens when missionaries convert natives.)[27]

A world picture is a basis or framework within which other beliefs are grounded and are accepted, rejected, replaced, judged to be true or false, or left undecided. Wittgenstein uses a variety of metaphors to describe the nature of a world picture. He sometimes compares it to a "river-bed of our thoughts," a "scaffolding," an "unused siding." Like the arrangement of twigs in a nest, the components of a world picture mutually support one another, and, in doing so, provide grounds or supports for any items that may come to "rest within" or "upon" them. He writes:

> As children we learn facts: e.g., that every human being has a brain, and we take them on trust. I believe there is an island, Australia, of such-and-such a shape, and so on and so on; I believe that I had great-grandparents, that the people who gave themselves out as my parents really were my parents, etc. This belief may never have been expressed; even the thought that it was so, never thought.
>
> I have a telephone conversation with New York. My friend tells me that his young trees have buds of such and such a kind. I am now convinced that his tree is. . . . Am I also convinced that the earth exists?
>
> In general, I take as true what is found in text-books, of geography for example. Why? All these facts have been confirmed a hundred times over. But how do I know that? What is my evidence for it? I have a world picture. Is it true or false? Above all it is the substratum of all my enquiring and asserting. The propositions describing it are not all equally subject to testing.
>
> I believe that every human being has two human parents; but Catholics believe that Jesus only had a human mother.

[27] *On Certainty*, secs. 608–612.

And other people might believe that there are human beings with no parents, and give no credence to all the contrary evidence. Catholics believe as well that in certain circumstances a wafer completely changes its nature, and at the same time that all evidence proves the contrary. And so if Moore said "I know that this is wine and not blood," Catholics would contradict him.[28]

The above examples, as well as others that may be adduced as characterizing some world picture or other, form a varied collection. Some are of an everyday sort that are virtually universal for human beings at all times and in all cultures. Others may have their source in specialized institutions of a culture, belong to particular stages of historical development, or are associated with distinctive individual and communal practices. For example, the belief that the Sun is the center of our planetary system is of scientific origin and commonly accepted. Such beliefs come to be accepted only at a certain stage of cultural development and are unlike other judgments that are still controversial or fluid. Still others—such as beliefs concerning the role of bread and wine in the celebration of the Mass—have their source in the tradition and practices of a particular religion. While the list of fixed and unquestioned beliefs may reveal some that are philosophical, the use of this label should not imply that it is the deposit of some process of reflection on the part of the individual accepting the belief. Having a world picture is part of the intellectual equipment of every human being, although over the course of the individual's lifetime parts of it may undergo change. Nor is the possession of a world picture restricted to those endowed with special gifts or those who are the beneficiaries of a specialized, professional training. Those classified as suffering from pathological, neurological, or psychiatric disorders have their own world pictures just as much as do others. The application of the term "world picture" is for purely descriptive purposes and is not intended to entail any evaluative judgment as to its "merit." The

[28] *On Certainty*, secs. 159, 208, 162, 239.

hallmark of any item or belief forming part of a world picture is the fact that for the person(s) holding that world picture there is an unquestioning acceptance of the beliefs comprising it. To unearth where each item in any particular world picture came from is not a simple matter, or even known by those who have the world picture. Some may have had their source in a long-forgotten myth or in some influential philosophic or theological scheme, in the channeled training of home or school, or as the fruit of common or expert observational experience, and so on. The particular mix of contents and sources will vary as one surveys different world pictures, despite the presence of some overlapping and sharing of certain items. Variations could be ascribed to differences in and relative strength of component cultural institutions, personal experience, education, and the like.

Consider a biochemist's use of the phrase "I know" in the statement "I know this is wine and not blood" when asked to analyze the liquid contained in the priest's chalice while performing Holy Communion. We should normally take his use of the words "I know" to mean that he expects confidence to be placed in his ability to make this kind of judgment, and that he has made the appropriate experiments or observations. The result he reaches is formulated as an empirically warranted proposition. On the other hand, if, in describing Holy Communion, a Catholic were to say "I know this is blood, not wine," the phrase "I know" in this context does not have the same use as it does for the chemist. The certainty and knowledge claimed for this statement has nothing to do with technical *scientific* expertise: it is not an empirically warranted judgment. It has to do with a component of a world picture that has a particular religious character.

In general, then, in considering the cognitive status of a belief it is important to determine whether it functions as part of a world picture or in some other capacity, for one and the same verbal expression of a belief may function in either way. It may be part of an established world picture or occupy a fluid status in ongoing empirical science, or be used in some special circumstance of everyday life where it might be appropriate to entertain doubts or investigate whether it is true. With a particular sentence or belief, taken in isolation, one cannot tell where it belongs. Thus such simple statements as "I have two hands" or "This is a tree," while normally classified as empirical statements, function differently when they serve as unquestioned parts of a world picture. At a particular stage of history in the life of a community, certain factual claims may still be subject to doubt and inquiry, part of "the flowing river," whereas at another stage they may have become fossilized, part of the bedrock or riverbank of a world picture. Conversely, what for a long time may have been part of the riverbank may (for various reasons) become loosened, dislodged, and once more fluid. At one time, it was thought impossible for men to walk on the Moon; today we know differently.

From the above summary, it is clear that a world picture is in some respects like a grammar, a norm of representation. It too is not to be judged as true or false, although it serves as a basis for judging other statements as true or false. Are there other similarities as well as significant differences between world pictures and grammatical rules? It is to a consideration of this important question that we turn next.

As we have seen, a principal feature of Wittgenstein's later philosophy of language is the doctrine of the *autonomy of grammar*. The creation of grammatical rules is a human activity that sets the bounds of sense. In this activity, men are free and not beholden to some supposed constraints "in reality": "Grammar is not accountable to any reality. It is grammatical rules that determine meaning (constitute it) and so they themselves are not answerable to any meaning and to that extent are arbitrary."[29] Despite such autonomy, the rules by themselves are unable to determine what is true or false. While one must first satisfy the grammatical rules of a language in making a meaningful descriptive statement, the determination of the truth or falsity of the statement is not established by consulting those grammatical rules. That is a matter for experience to settle, of finding out what

[29] *Philosophical Grammar*, sec. 133.

the facts are. In the case of understanding the role of grammar as constituting a set of norms of representation that determine the bounds of sense, we can be reasonably clear in most cases about how to distinguish a rule of grammar from an empirical proposition. As distinguished from sentences that *formulate* grammatical rules, empirical propositions involve the *application* of grammatical rules in particular circumstances, and, as such, can be evaluated as true or false. This evaluation is not a matter of understanding or explaining the meaning of grammatical rules but of establishing whether the application of the rules in empirical propositions agrees with what is found in experience. Thus grammar may give us rules about the meaning of the terms "red" or "length," but they do not settle whether *this* confronted object or surface is to be correctly described as being red, or whether this rod, when measured, is ten feet long. For that we must find out what holds "in reality": we must perform observations or measurements and let these guide our decision.

Let us now consider the status of world pictures. Can we make sense of an "autonomy of world pictures" in the same way in which we spoke of an "autonomy of grammar"? If the answer is in the affirmative—that is, if we say that the creation and adoption of world pictures is a human prerogative and a distinctively human activity and possession, and that the groundlessness of world pictures is another way of stressing their autonomy—is there any sense in considering the *application* of world pictures, as there is in the case of grammar? We saw that despite the latter's autonomy, grammatical rules are by themselves unable to settle questions of truth or falsity: for that, one must turn "to reality." Is there any reality to which one can apply a world picture?

Wittgenstein maintains that while it is appropriate and relevant to inquire about the truth or falsity of "fluid" empirical judgments—to ask about their evidence and degree of certainty (probability)—it makes no sense to apply these normative terms to the judgments, beliefs, and propositions that constitute a world picture. He writes:

But I did not get my picture of the world by satisfying myself of its correctness; nor do I have it because I am satisfied of its correctness. No: it is the inherited background against which I distinguish between true and false.

The propositions describing the world picture might be part of a kind of mythology. And their role is like that of rules of a game; and the game can be learned purely practically, without learning any explicit rules.[30]

And again:

What prevents me from supposing that this table either vanishes or alters its shape and colour when no one is observing it, and then when someone looks at it again changes back to its old condition?—"But who is going to suppose such a thing!"—one would feel like saying.

Here we see that the idea of 'agreement with reality' does not have any clear application.[31]

Should we say, therefore, that world pictures, unlike the application of grammatical rules in the case of empirical propositions, are *not* open to evaluation by reality? In that case, it would not make sense to apply a world picture in the expectation that one might appeal to something beyond the world picture to determine its acceptability. If it is indeed the case that "one of the deepest and most pervasive errors in philosophy [is] predicating of the world what lies in our method of representation (*Darstellungsweise*),"[32] then what are we to understand of the

---

[30] *On Certainty*, secs. 94, 95.

[31] *On Certainty*, secs. 214, 215.

[32] P.M.S. Hacker, *Insight and Illusion: Wittgenstein on Philosophy and the Metaphysics of Experience* (Oxford: Clarendon Press, 1972), 150; cf. with the following: "There is no way of 'thinking' reality except by means of representation. Yet it is the form of representation we employ which determines reality and what forms it has. One cannot conceptualize without concepts and hence one cannot in general justify a conceptual scheme by reference to reality as described in terms of that scheme. What I take to be reality is not independent of, but is logically related to my conceptual scheme" (ibid., 164).

use, here, of the term "the world" in the expression "world picture"? Is not the very term "world picture" itself responsible for this confusion, since it is obviously based on analogy with other "pictures" and their "objects"?

One way of regarding Wittgenstein's view of what response to make to the question concerning the "relation between world pictures—treated as schemes of representation—and reality" is that the question is a pseudo-question. It is another version of the quest for *metaphysical knowledge*. It presupposes there is a reality and therefore that we can legitimately ask what that reality is. We are inclined to regard reality as an "object." In line with an "Augustinian picture of language," we regard reality as the referent of a name. And we also would agree with Plato who believed this "object" has its own essence, and that we can ask what that essence is. But for Wittgenstein this is a misleading picture and a fruitless way of dealing with the expression "reality." He writes: "I read '. . . philosophers are no nearer to the meaning of "Reality" than Plato got, . . .' What a strange situation. How extraordinary that Plato could have got even as far as he did! Or that we could not get any further! Was it because Plato was so *extremely* clever?"[33]

When it comes to *empirical knowledge*, one cannot know by grammar alone. The latter establishes the bounds or conditions of sense or meaning, and to know the truth, one needs more than sense or meaning. However, world pictures do not give *metaphysical knowledge*. And if one asks how to determine the truth or falsity of a world picture, Wittgenstein would respond by saying one is asking a confused, pseudo-question. It fails to understand that a world picture cannot be evaluated in terms of its truth or falsity. It presumes that a world picture can be judged in terms of its success in giving metaphysical knowledge of the world: of reality. However, one can only *act* in terms of a world picture, but one cannot *know* by means of (or through) it. Thus Wittgen-

---

[33] Wittgenstein, *Culture and Value* (Oxford: Basil Blackwell, 1980), 15.

stein would reject the question posed. The procedure is nonsensical and self-defeating because it is circular.

Wittgenstein's account of what it is to be a world picture suggests that the nature of such a picture is not made by confronting the world independently and then drawing a picture of it, and such that one may look at both and see how faithful, adequate, or true the picture is. On the contrary, one is limited to the picture. If one does use the term "world," it is what is so characterized in a particular world picture. The world is what a world picture says it is. The expression "the world" is a term whose sense is explained by bringing in other terms or concepts, and not by going outside the explanation as given *in* language.

Would Wittgenstein wish to say, then, that world pictures *create* reality? Is he a "world picture idealist"?[34] Or does he uphold some form of "realism"? Does he subscribe to the view that quite independently of our world pictures there is a reality about which we might at least raise the question of whether—or to what extent, if any—there is a legitimate question of the relation of the representations making up the world picture to it? What sort of relation is it, if not a matter of truth? In reply, I suggest, Wittgenstein would repudiate both the labels "idealist" or "realist," since they represent classifications with respect to differences concerning metaphysical knowledge, and therefore are vacuous and to be rejected. There are as many "worlds" as there are world pictures.

Let us substitute the term "reality" for Wittgenstein's term "world." Then one important consequence of his account of world pictures (reality pictures) is that we have no "access" to reality as that which putatively exists independently of, antecedently to, and "in itself," apart from all pictures, because the very supposition of the meaningfulness of such possible "access" is incoherent and to be rejected. The question of judging the truth or

---

[34] For contrasting viewpoints on this theme, see Bernard Williams, "Wittgenstein and Idealism," in Godfrey Vesey, ed., *Understanding Wittgenstein* (Ithaca, N.Y.: Cornell University Press, 1974), 76–95; Norman Malcolm, "Wittgenstein and Idealism," in Godfrey Vesey, ed., *Idealism Past and Present* (Cambridge, Eng.: Cambridge University Press, 1982), 249–267.

adequacy of any world picture is a question that cannot be answered, not because we have no way of knowing what the world or reality is in-itself, but because the very presupposition that there is such a possible object or subject matter is one that cannot be accepted. And this would make all efforts futile at evaluating world pictures by matching them against a putative reality. For the very use of the term "reality," in stating such a presumed project, already presupposes its use according to a conception drawn in one or another world picture. And one cannot match a picture against itself, to determine its "truth."

For Wittgenstein there is no "in itself," no hidden, *unknowable* reality that is inaccessible to world pictures. Unlike Kant, Wittgenstein does not make any reference to any hidden reality, any noumenal realm, whose existence he acknowledges. On the recommended philosophy, we cannot think of the world as containing some inherent structure or hidden essence of its own, for to use this way of speaking is obviously to commit the very philosophic fallacy we are being warned against. "Inherent structure" and "(hidden) essence" are humanly created forms of representation, though not applicable to what may be assumed to be features belonging to the world "in itself."

The Wittgensteinian thesis concerning world pictures negates the possibility of achieving *metaphysical knowledge* of reality. It challenges the legitimacy of engaging in any discussion that would hope to settle claims entered on behalf of any preferred world picture. It excludes the possibility of making any noncircular appeal to criteria or neutral method for judging the comparative merits of any world picture that would involve appealing to the "essence" of the world for determining the "truth" about reality. In one way, the outcome of this analysis and the message it leaves us with involve a surrender of all hope of having a theory of reality other than by "persuasion." All pictures are in the same boat, and there is no sense in asking for a "sound," "correct," or "true" world picture. Even the distinction between a proposition establishing a purely conceptual connection (as in a grammatical rule) and an empirical proposition—a distinction so important in

Wittgenstein's later philosophy, that would also be of importance to any philosophy relying on science as the preferred method for achieving knowledge of the universe—is itself the expression of a particular world picture, in the Wittgensteinian sense.

For Wittgenstein, in short, there is no independent metaphysical reality to get to! Hence any attempt to judge how close or far Plato's account, or any other, is, as a metaphysical system, to disclosing the essence of reality is a mirage, a futile project. To draw a parallel between rules of grammar and world pictures in this respect is a mistake and philosophically confused. For it presumes that one can look for metaphysical knowledge in a fashion parallel to the legitimacy of looking for *empirical knowledge.* While the doctrine of the autonomy of grammar forbids treating the status of grammar as a form of empirical knowledge, it nevertheless leaves room for obtaining genuine instances of the latter through the application of grammatical rules. However, the status of world pictures is different in this respect from grammar. Even though we might affirm the autonomy of world pictures, there is no sense in the supposition that we might apply a world picture to obtain an example of *metaphysical knowledge.* This would presume there is a reality that lies "beyond" our world pictures that exists independently of our world pictures and that "it" has a certain set of inherent properties and essence. This presupposition must be surrendered. The autonomy of world pictures is all we have. World pictures are embedded in forms of life, but cannot be judged by comparison with some independent entity by means of some universally accepted criterion or by some neutral method and fund of evidence. There is nothing to compare world pictures with. One can only compare one world picture with other world pictures, not with something that is not a world picture—something which we may wish to designate as "reality"! And this marks a major difference between the autonomy of grammar and the autonomy of world pictures.

If we omit or exclude, as we presumably must on this orientation, what language and various forms of representation *project* on the world but do not *inhere* in the world, what is left to the world "in itself" apart from human creative projections and forms of representation? It would seem either we must retreat altogether to silence in "referring" to the world, or else cease drawing a crude distinction between the world (or reality) and world pictures!

Part 2

o o o

BETWEEN AN
ANSWER AND
NO ANSWER

FOUR

What Is Reality?

It is time to pause and gather the fruits of our discussion thus far. We will take advantage of the surveys made and the critical judgments passed; we will amplify the positive clues we have found about where to look for an answer to the question of reality, or give reasons for surrendering any hope of finding one.

INTELLIGIBILITY

In approaching a discussion of the question of reality, we do well to begin not with reality on its most comprehensive scale, but with a much narrower subject matter: ourselves. For we have in our own makeup a feature that, depending on how it is exercised, plays a crucial role in influencing both the direction in which metaphysical world views of the widest scope will be sought and, when found, the shape these views will take. Not unexpectedly, the feature of our own makeup that plays this important role in affecting the character of metaphysical views has to do with what Aristotle long ago recognized in his definition of the essence of man: the power to exercise reason.

What it is to be "rational" is a complex topic, rich in controversy. For present purposes, however, we need not penetrate that complexity beyond pointing out, in an elementary way, that to be rational is connected with such closely related matters as (1) the capacity for intellectual comprehension: a capacity manifested in the use of abstract concepts and general patterns of thought; (2) the exercise of creative imagination and practical intelligence in the choice of means to achieve chosen ends; and (3) the trained and skilled use of language for communication. These are different strands in the multifaceted functioning of reason, though they are closely intertwined with one another. Of course, each of them, taken separately, invites specialized consideration of its own distinctive features—a challenge that fuels the inexhaustible drive toward finding ever better ways of providing this analysis.

However, if we were to look for some single theme that, despite the individual character and emphasis of each strand, nevertheless shows the strands to be inextricably linked as aspects of one and the same "faculty of reason," it is not likely that we should find a better way of doing this than by pointing to the omnipresent interest human beings have in finding, establishing, appreciating, or communicating some example or type of *intelligible order*. In a broad and generous sense, to say that something is intelligible is to say that it can be understood, that it has a structure or order, and that thereby in some degree it satisfies our need as rational beings in finding such order. In serving this concern with intelligible order, whether in our own lives or in the world around us, reason therefore devotes a good deal of attention, both on a personal level and through the agency of various cultural institutions, to articulating what it takes to be the manifold conditions, activities, and methods that make it possible for such order to be formulated, recognized, established, enjoyed, and communicated.

Crucial to this notion of rationality as intelligibility are two fundamental features: (1) that the order or structure rendered intelligible is linked, in some way, with the activity of a conscious being; and (2) that insofar as intelligibility is to be found in or introduced into a subject matter, it is the result of discerning various specific relations or combinations among various discriminated objects, factors, or elements in that subject matter. There are, of course, many variations on this basic schema, variations that one finds in the rich histories of philosophy, theology, and science, from ancient times to the present.

In this book, we have explored, in particular, two major examples of this schema. One of the chief results of this exploration that has importance to our further inquiry concerns the distinction between the Platonic and Kantian views of the concept of intelligibility when considered in the context of reaching a general view concerning the nature of reality, and associated differences concerning the possibility of achieving such metaphysical knowledge.

Before turning to considering afresh the question of reality and the prospects of answering it, while yet fully aware of the possible attractions and influences of our inherited guidelines, let me briefly summarize the major differences between these two approaches to the concept of intelligibility. This concept, along with the concept of existence, will play a major role in the analysis to follow.

1. Plato's attempt in the *Timaeus* to account for the intelligibility of the universe relies on the model of rational art as practiced by a Cosmic Craftsman. This Platonic approach to the concept of intelligibility is the predominant one in the history of philosophy, although it is by no means confined to Plato's own formulation and its various details, nor is it always identified as such in its general form. The impact of this orientation to the notion of intelligibility is found at different historical epochs in manifold variations—whether in science, religion, or philosophy. Two main directions of such influences on a cosmic and metaphysical level are relevant to our special interest: both are crucial examples of reason's preoccupation with order and intelligibility. It is this way of thinking that finds its ready support in the explicit reliance on the analogy of "rational art" in various transformed and attenuated schemes of theology. Its wide-ranging influence is felt as well, though more remotely, in numerous philosophical accounts and individual scientist's credos of the goals and achievements of science. We have taken note, earlier,

of some of these specific influences and repercussions of Plato's thought. One direction of application of this concern is especially evident in those systems of metaphysics and theology that explain the existence of the world: in solving the mystery of existence. The other direction of application is manifested in the prevalent ambitions of science to discover the inherent intelligible structure in Nature that would completely explain the occurrence of observed phenomena. The first type of interest in intelligibility looks for an explanation of the very existence of the world as an ordered structure. The other looks for appropriate conceptual means by which to articulate and give a true account of that ordered structure, and thereby explain its individual observed instances.

According to this general Platonic view, when articulations of intelligible order are credited with being true it is because the proposed articulations match the way things are in reality. Reality as knowable already has, prior to human investigation, its own lines of division among factors, elements, entities, or objects: its own structural patterns of interrelation and order. The goal of human efforts at achieving knowledge and truth should therefore be seen as devoted to finding out what these components and order are and giving them correct, suitable reference and inclusion in an acceptable description. This, roughly, is the realist's epistemological credo; it is a crucial component of the Platonic heritage. It is the common thread that, shared in one form or another, underlies and recurs down through the ages in various programs and schemes of theology, philosophy, and science.

Since, on this approach, the achievement of knowledge and truth consists in a matching between human concepts and what exists (putatively) in reality, it makes most sense to think of the matching as involving two sets of concepts. On the one hand, there are those concepts that are fashioned by, conveyed in language by, and variously used by human beings; and, on the other hand, there are those "objective" concepts (for example, Plato's Forms) that enjoy their own independent, extrahuman ontological status, and are exemplified or instantiated through reality's own divisions and structuring. "Matching" implies finding something similar or identical in what is being matched. Hence, in the quest for knowledge and truth, if we look for what matches some particular set of human concepts and linguistic expressions, one should look for that to which they come closest in character. If these are not simply other human concepts, they will have to be of an extrahuman or superhuman character and source.

The foregoing summary of epistemological realism holds not only for Plato's *Timaeus*, but for various of its many offshoots and analogs. Its hold on our thought has been so great that many will take its principles as being no more than the most obvious deliverances of common sense, hence as belonging to the unquestioned foundations of any world picture that may offer itself as a candidate for our acceptance.

2. The other main approach to the concept of intelligibility is linked to the innovative aspects of the Kantian revolution and to its various subsequent modifications and adaptations in the history of modern philosophy. Even if one cannot accept all the details of Kant's own formulation of the philosophy of transcendental idealism (with its emphasis on a fixed, universal, cognitive apparatus belonging to the human mind), the main emphasis of the Kantian revolution in its criticism of traditional realism persists in the thought of various individual thinkers, subsidiary movements, and phases of modern philosophy. It is discernible, for example, in the philosophy of language of Wittgenstein's later writings.

The chief difference between this general approach to intelligibility and the Platonic one is that the articulation of order attributed to reality is the result of bringing to bear schemes of intelligibility whose origin is the creative exercise of human consciousness, not that of a Divine Mind. Crucial to this view is the rejection of any belief in the objective existence of a unique, intelligible structure that preexists the application of the conceptual or linguistic schemes introduced by human beings, or a claim to be able to appraise possible scientific or metaphysical knowledge in terms of a correspondence between the human sources of conceptual understanding and the putatively existing, unique, intelligible order in reality or the world "in itself."

On Wittgenstein's version of this broad Kantian orientation, intelligibility is made possible by bringing to bear humanly devised grammars in the interest of describing and explaining the materials of human experience. All concepts are human creations. Where successful, the application of these human conceptual schemes does not disclose some antecedently existing, inherent, unique intelligible pattern in the world, but confers intelligibility upon the materials of experience by selecting among various ways of articulating an intelligible structure in such material. There is no possible appeal to what "Nature" or "phenomena" themselves tell us is the case, without the application of such ineliminable, humanly creative conceptual factors.

For Wittgenstein, there is an important distinction between the appeal to observation for purposes of extralinguistic reference and determination of truth, as contrasted with the explanation of the *meaning* of humanly created linguistic rules. Rules have their sanction in human stipulation, in the autonomy of human decision. It is the application, not the explanation of the meaning of a grammatical rule, that requires going outside the rules themselves to what is found in observation, and thus to what is not a matter of human creativity or decision. It is we human beings who create conceptual bounds and use them. We devise languages and grammatical rules, and apply them to all sorts of subject matters with results that display varying degrees of success. While many conceptual schemes, or parts thereof, are common to many cultures and throughout human history, others are more specialized, limited in their use and comprehension, or prevalent only at certain stages of history or in some certain special communities and cultures. In any case, what is distinctive about human beings is their capacity for flexibility in their activity of making, changing, and choosing among their multiple conceptual schemes.

Nor can the choice among differing conceptual schemes or

grammars be determined by looking to find which is preferred and already embodied in Nature. A subject matter interpreted with the aid of a grammar becomes intelligible not by making explicit what was there all along in the subject matter, but by introducing ways of saying in what the intelligible order consists. Since there are many actual or possible grammars and conceptual schemes, there are different ways of achieving this. Preferences are determined by making comparisons among available conceptual schemes and by pragmatic considerations. For Wittgenstein, the application of grammatical rules for scientific cognitive purposes requires appeal to observational experience to determine what can be said to hold of reality. But if one asks what is the nature of reality "in itself" that does not depend on the use of language, or on an appeal to observational experience, or on the guidance of a preferred world picture, Wittgenstein would dismiss the question on the grounds that it is meaningless and incoherent. To speak of what reality on any level or in any of its components is "in itself" has no sense. For every attempt to think or say *what* something is involves language and its humanly devised grammar or accepted world picture. Take away the grammatical rules and the world picture and the "what" evaporates, dissolves. It cannot be said or be thought of because there is nothing to be said or thought of. What "things" are "in themselves" is unsayable, unknowable, and unintelligible, but not because of any incompetence or limitations on the part of human beings.

To sum up this general Kantian view of intelligibility, especially in the light of Wittgenstein's reformulation, we might say the following. With the aid of the conceptual bounds created in ordinary language, myths, science, and philosophy, human beings practice various types of "rational art," or what they think of as such. But all of this belongs to us as existent parts of the universe. In applying our conceptual creations to rendering the universe and its contents intelligible, some applications turn out to be better than others—not, however, because they match some inherent, unique, intelligible pattern that preexists in the world, but because we make comparative evaluations among available ways of ordering, and introduce preferences and rankings among them in terms of how well we think they help us to explain, predict, enlarge, and, in general, deal "successfully" with experience. In short, we *confer* intelligibility upon our experience of the world. It is man, the rational craftsman, who makes the world, as he experiences it, intelligible according to his own lights.

FORMULATING THE QUESTION OF REALITY

In turning next to an attempt at our own formulation of "the question of reality," let us begin by asking whether it is one that might profitably be formulated by means of a standard sentence-frame of an interrogative sort, as distinguished from other types of sentence-frames in everyday language—for example, declarative, imperative, exhortatory, or exclamatory. Among the variety of interrogative frames, it appears initially plausible to formulate the question of reality as asking, *"What* is reality?" Let us consider what is involved in adopting this suggestion.

One use of the "What is . . . ?" type of question looks for a way of identifying an individual entity as the sought-for referent of a nominative expression. If we follow this use, we would transform the expression "reality" into the proper name "Reality" and regard its use as comparable to using a proper name for an individual object or substance—for example, a planet. One of the commonly assumed features of a nonproblematic use of a name for an individual is that, when successfully employed, it will serve to pick out, to identify, the individual being referred to. Pluto is one of the planets, the Empire State Building is one of the buildings in New York City. Furthermore, the ordinary use of a proper name presupposes that the individual object referred to is a member of a class in which one might identify other actual or possible individuals. Even if one assumes or claims that it is unique by virtue of its possession of certain properties (for example, in the case of a planet, in being farthest from the Sun), we should normally say that the application of these predicates as descriptions of these properties might be mistaken. Perhaps Pluto is not the planet farthest from the Sun: it is conceivable that some other planet is entitled to that description.

However, if we are tempted to use the expression "Reality" as a name for an individual entity, does its use allow the existence of other actual or possible individual entities in some superclass that embraces both Reality and other individuals? This would subvert one general use of the term "Reality" in metaphysical contexts. This cautionary remark is perhaps sufficient to discourage the use of the expression "Reality" as a name for an individual entity in the way we would ordinarily use a proper name. A readiness to disregard this cautionary remark could be taken as another example of the common propensity to follow the prototypical "Augustinian picture of language" by treating all words as names for objects or entities of one sort or another.

In face of the foregoing demurrer at unhesitatingly treating the term "reality" in metaphysical contexts as equivalent to the capitalized expression "Reality" to serve as a proper name for a concrete individual object or entity, there is another line of thought that might seem more appropriate at first glance: to regard it as an abstract noun that can be analyzed as having a primarily predicative role. Consider, for example, the case of "rectangularity." If we were to ask "What is rectangularity?" a first helpful step would be to replace the nominative expression with a predicative one. We should then consider statements of the form "x is rectangular." One way of explaining the meaning of "rectangular" is to offer a definition that lists its essential characteristics—for example, "to have the shape of a closed plane figure with four right angles." Another type of explanation employs an ostensive type of definition: it gives an example of the shape by pointing to it, thereby incorporating the example as part of the rule explaining its meaning. Having mastered these and other types of grammatical rules that explain the meaning of "rectangular," we could then use the predicate "rectangular" to describe some object, drawing, and so forth.

If we take the foregoing as a guide for dealing with the term "reality," the first step would be to replace the nominative expression "reality" by the predicative expression "real," and then look for ways of explaining its meaning in sentences of the form "*x* is real." Among such uses, we might point to two: in one sense, to say "*x* is real" is another way of saying "*x actually exists* and is not a fiction." In another use, to say "*x* is real" is to say "*x* is *genuine* and not a fake." That these are distinct uses can be seen from the fact that if something actually exists it does not follow that it is also genuine: a fake object (one that is *not* real in this sense) nevertheless may be real in the sense that it actually exists and is not fictional. Of these two uses of "real," the use "actually exists" could be selected for its greater relevance to an inquiry of a general metaphysical sort, such as we are here concerned with, since the other use of "real" has a highly limited use only in connection with certain social practices and artifacts. Of course, once we have made this substitution of "actually exists" for "real," we have not gained very much, since the meanings of "exists," "actually exists," or close cognates are extremely diverse both in ordinary language and in the specialized vocabularies of philosophy.[1] There is no general consensus with respect to the use of "exists," any more than there is with respect to the use of the terms "truth" or "reality."

Neither of the foregoing routes that would follow a standard way for interpreting the use of the "What is . . . ?" sentence-frame is, accordingly, a promising one for raising the question of reality. That question cannot be taken as unequivocally and non-controversially voicing either a request for the identification of an individual concrete entity or object referred to by a proper name, or an interest in finding some set of defining properties that underlies the predicative use of an abstract noun. If there is a genuine question to be raised or answered, and if we persist in using standard sentence-frames for raising the question—and in partic-

---

[1] Cf. the valuable series of studies, under the general editorship of John W. M. Verhaar, *The Verb 'Be' and Its Synonyms: Philosophical and Grammatical Studies* (Dordrecht-Holland: Reidel, 1967), Foundations of Language/Supplementary Series.

ular the "What" form of question—we must be prepared to recognize very strong exceptions, qualifications, and limitations in the use of such ordinary ways of addressing the question—unless, of course, we are convinced that there are so many exceptions, qualifications, and limitations that it is a wiser choice to give up altogether the project of framing the question of reality in ordinary language. For some, therefore, the question evaporates as meaningless because it is not even capable of being clearly formulated, much less answered.

Instead of adopting the latter view, many have held the view that there is some room for maneuverability in the treatment of the question, and that in the presence of this opportunity, once found, there are some tactics that might be employed within the degrees of freedom allowed. Thus, if we are convinced that the use of the expression "Reality" as a name for a concrete individual entity is to be avoided, we might nevertheless wish to retain this capitalized expression as a name whose intended referent is recognized to be so absolutely unique and all-encompassing that it is necessary to acknowledge at the very outset that "what it is" cannot be identified by ordinary techniques or described by means of ordinary predicative expressions. One cannot point to Reality or use any form of ostension, nor can one give a literal description of it. If Reality is absolutely unique, any apprehension of it must be made either in silence, as in some form of *satori* (awakening), or, if in language and by means of "concepts," this can be done only in some very special and restricted way. For there are no ordinary concepts (being general and therefore available for application and reapplication to multiple instances) that apply directly, affirmatively, and uniquely to Reality.

In the face of this, we can consider the options of using language *metaphorically*, or, if we use predicates taken from ordinary language, we should use them only in *negative* statements, that is, in statements that exclude Reality from the range of subjects to which such predicates can be normally and meaningfully applied. Reality is "not this, not that"; it is "wholly other."

There is, however, a third option. Besides using ordinary general terms in a very strongly metaphoric way, or—where the subject is Reality—using ordinary predicates but only in negative statements, we can isolate special uses of the term "existence" and apply them directly and literally in stating crucial parts of the "groundless" principles of a distinctive world picture. I propose to adopt this latter course, and shall concentrate my discussion on two major strands in the use of the term "exists" (or its nominalization).

One of these meanings comes to the fore insofar as the universe, in its existence as one dimension of Reality, can be inquired into, described, and rendered in some degree intelligible. The achievement of such intelligibility involves the use of conceptual bounds devised and applied by human beings. By contrast with the foregoing, I employ the other meaning of the term "exists"—"Boundless Existence"—to designate a dimension of Reality that is not open to the successful application of any humanly devised conceptual schemes: Boundless Existence is unintelligible. It does not yield to any inquiry that can result in genuine metaphysical knowledge, any more than it is a subject matter open to scientific inquiry.

FIVE

The Universe

DOES THE UNIVERSE EXIST?

The belief that the universe exists is probably as widely shared a belief as one is likely to find. To deny or even challenge it is not only to fly in the face of the most elementary and universal common sense, but also to suspect the sanity of one who does so. Accordingly, while many will admit that some of their other beliefs have succumbed to a critical attack that caused a belief to be abandoned or greatly modified, the belief that the universe exists is surely impervious to such dislodgment. In order to forestall any possible misunderstandings and to try to overcome the possibly strong resistance that many might feel at even being invited to consider the question "Does the universe exist?" let me begin by showing why I believe its analysis raises issues of genuine philosophic importance.

The first point to be made is that, without further clarification of the possible ways of interpreting the question along with the key terms in it, it cannot be adequately answered with a simple "yes" or "no." To fulfill this initial requirement is to take a long step toward recasting the initial statement of the question into a more specific and tractable form. Having accomplished this, we may then set about considering arguments in support of giving a definite negative or positive answer, or indeed acknowledging, for some particular versions of the question, that it may not be possible for various reasons to give a determinate affirmative or negative answer at all.

To the foregoing comment, someone might say: "I don't accept your suggestion that I consider various senses of the terms 'universe' and 'exists,' or that I be prepared to modify or abandon my belief that the universe exists. I have a direct, unshakable, and immediate knowledge of both the meaning and truth of my belief that the universe exists."

To this, the response should be: "Language is an instrument for communication, and the meanings of its expressions should not be regarded as established or certified in a wholly private way. What meanings we are asked to attach to expressions should rest upon publicly accessible procedures and rules. You may propose to give the terms 'the universe' and 'exists' whatever meanings you choose, provided we know what they are. But, then, if you regard the statement 'The universe exists' as unshakably or necessarily true, it is not because you have captured something that is factually true, but only because you have used the sentence to make a linguistic recommendation in the form either of a definition or an identity statement. In the first case, what you offer is only a proposal to adopt a certain grammatical rule about the term 'universe,' according to which 'exists' is treated as belonging to the definiens of 'universe.' In that case, we are at liberty to adopt or reject your proposal. On the other hand, if you regard the terms 'universe' and 'existence' as wholly synonymous or interchangeable, then the entire sentence is an identity statement, and again, therefore, it functions as a linguistic recommendation. In short, your so-called unshakable belief is only a recommendation about the use of two linguistic expressions: 'the universe' and 'exists' (or 'existence'). In either case, your so-called belief is not either true or false, and therefore does not contribute to or communicate any form of factual knowledge."

There is a curious argument of a rather different sort from the foregoing that might also discourage a consideration of the question, "Does the universe exist?" This time, however, instead of dismissing the question as not worth considering because the answer, "The universe exists," is allegedly so obvious, the opposite view is held that the very concept "universe" is one we no longer have any need for! It was Bertrand Russell who once made this latter suggestion. In his essay "On Scientific Method in Philosophy," he wrote:

> I believe the conception of "the universe" to be, as its etymology indicates, a mere relic of pre-Copernican astronomy. . . . In the days before Copernicus, the conception of the "universe" was defensible on scientific grounds: the diurnal revolution of the heavenly bodies bound them together as all parts of one system, of which the earth was the centre. Round this apparent scientific fact, many human desires rallied: the wish to believe Man important in the scheme of things, the theoretical desire for a comprehensive understanding of the Whole, the hope that the course of nature might be guided by some sympathy with our wishes. . . . When Copernicus swept away the astronomical basis of this system of thought, it had grown so familiar, and had associated itself so intimately with men's aspirations, that it survived with scarcely diminished force—survived even Kant's "Copernican revolution," and is still now the unconscious premiss of most metaphysical systems.[1]

In the foregoing comment, Russell obviously ignores the kind of interest scientific cosmologists have had and continue to have in using the concept or term "universe" without linking it exclusively to a pre-Copernican geocentric cosmology. For example, the ancient Democritean cosmology employed a concept of the universe that was neither geocentric, anthropocentric, nor astronomically finite. And, of course, modern scientific cosmology finds use for the term "universe" in connection with a great variety of cosmological models in which this use is by no means tied to the requirement that the universe be pictured as finite and

---

[1] Bertrand Russell, *Mysticism and Logic*, 2d ed. (London: Allen and Unwin, 1917), 98–99.

geocentric. But even when we take these obvious historical facts into account, it is crucial to distinguish a *grammatical rule* that explains the use of the term "universe" from the *factual truth or falsity* of an astronomical theory in which it may be employed. The fact that geocentric pre-Copernican cosmological theories have been discarded in no way undermines the foregoing distinction. Whatever be the fate of the factual truth of geocentric theories, the term "universe" continues to have wide employment in accordance with various rules for its use. This surely clears the way for considering different uses of the term and for focusing our attention on how to respond to the question, "Does the universe exist?"

The use of the term "universe," like any other term in common or technical use, is context-relative. It does not have a single, well-defined use that is universally recognized and is totally isolated from being embedded in a network of other expressions, or of being employed in the course of pursuing some special interest. Thus one recognized way of using the expression "the universe" is to refer to the sum total of whatever exists or has being ("the world at large"); another, somewhat narrower use is to refer to the totality of those entities that have *physical* existence. Those who use the expression "the universe" in either of these senses normally have a philosophical, theological, or metaphysical interest in making use of these meanings, and they are typically concerned with analyzing and finding interrelations among such concepts as "totality," "existence," "physical being," "levels of existence," and so on.

Related to the foregoing uses of the term "the universe" is the way some philosophers employ the term "cosmology." For example, the subtitle of A. N. Whitehead's major work, *Process and Reality*, is *An Essay in Cosmology*. In this work, Whitehead makes clear that he uses the term "cosmology" to mean "speculative philosophy," and this he defines as "the endeavour to frame a coherent, logical, necessary system of general ideas in terms of which every element of our experience can be interpreted. By this notion of 'interpretation' I mean that everything of which we are conscious, as enjoyed, perceived, willed, or thought, shall have the character of a particular instance of the general scheme."[2]

However, even if we were to share in some way the goals of this or other projects in metaphysics to achieve a satisfactory, comprehensive model of reality, there are other ways of using the expression "the universe" and conceiving of the scope of cosmology. Thus my own discussion, in what follows, focuses on the meanings of "universe" as used in the context of contemporary scientific cosmology. And while I shall thereby take a more restricted subject matter for examination than, say, Whitehead's, it will also serve as a fruitful if somewhat more indirect path for coming within sight of broader metaphysical goals.

In his article "The Universe as a Whole,"[3] British cosmologist Dennis W. Sciama asserts that "The existence of the universe is clearly its most important characteristic, but I am referring here to the stronger idea that it is meaningful to talk of the universe as a whole as a single well-defined concept. This idea is one of the most important, perhaps the most important, scientific discovery of the twentieth century."[4]

Since what Sciama says in support of the foregoing claim may enjoy wide agreement among many cosmologists or play its role in influencing the views of others, and since what he affirms goes to the heart of our present theme, it is of interest to pause for a detailed scrutiny of these few sentences.

1. Consider first the key terms used in the opening segment of the first sentence (viz., "The existence of the universe is clearly its most important characteristic"). They are that *existence* is a

---

[2] A. N. Whitehead, *Process and Reality: An Essay in Cosmology*, corrected edition, ed. D. R. Griffin and Donald W. Sherburne (New York: Free Press, 1978), 3.

[3] D. W. Sciama, "The Universe as a Whole," in J. Mehra ed., *The Physicist's Conception of Nature* (Dordrecht-Holland: Reidel, 1973), 17–33; cf. D. W. Sciama, *Modern Cosmology* (Cambridge, Eng.: Cambridge University Press, 1971), 98–101.

[4] Sciama, "The Universe as a Whole," 17.

characteristic (property) of the *universe*, and that among its characteristics, existence ranks as its *most important*. Behind the use of these highlighted terms we may readily discern a number of presuppositions: (a) the expression "the universe" can be used in a subject-predicate type of statement as the subject term to stand for something extralinguistic; (b) as the referent of the subject term, the universe has charactersitics or properties that inhere in or belong to it; (c) among these properties or characteristics is one labeled "existence"; the expression "existence," used predicatively, ascribes the property it stands for to the universe; (d) it makes sense to rank the properties of the universe with respect to their importance, and in such ranking the property of existence is most important.

Even if we grant that, taken at the level of the ordinary use of language, the quoted statement conveys what would be commonly or traditionally accepted as "true" and "obvious enough," there are connected with each of the aforementioned topics a number of philosophic controversies of serious and far-ranging import. From a philosophic point of view, one cannot afford to let these terms or the presuppositions that lie behind their use go unexamined. What can be said in favor of these presuppositions, or by contrast, for any challenges and alternatives to them? Of the various philosophic views thus brought to light, which, if any, should we adopt?

2. Consider, next, the claim that there is an even stronger idea than that of the existence of the universe, namely that "it is meaningful to talk of the universe as a whole as a single well-defined concept." (a) If, as seems to be implied, the concept of "the universe *as a whole*" (my italics) is to be distinguished from the expression "the universe"—where the latter is employed without the qualifying phrase "as a whole"—in what does the difference consist? What is added by the phrase "as a whole" that was not present in the use of the expression "the universe"? (b) If it can be shown that the concept of "the universe as a whole" is distinguishable from the use of the expression "the universe" as unqualified, what makes the former stronger? (c) Is it indeed the

case that the concept of the universe as a whole is well defined? According to what criteria? Are any of these to be preferred?

3. A third point made by Sciama is that the idea of the universe as a whole, as "a well-defined concept," "is one of the most important, perhaps the most important, scientific discovery of the twentieth century." (a) How does this claim square with the commonly accepted belief that the concept of the universe as a whole is one that was given meaning and employed as far back in human history as one is able to penetrate? (b) If indeed the concept of the universe as a whole, as employed in current scientific cosmology, is to be understood in a special sense as contrasted with traditional uses, in what way does this special sense constitute a discovery? What justifies the use of this expression in the present context? Is it comparable in certain familiar ways to other "discoveries"? Would it not be better, perhaps, to say that the concept of the universe as a whole is a creative, constructive achievement, an invention, not a discovery? (c) What makes the use of this concept in current cosmology the most important discovery of the twentieth century?

Having made what he recognizes to be the "grandiose claim" in the quoted sentences, Sciama proceeds to offer certain reservations. They are the following.

Various lines of thought in contemporary cosmology conceive of the possibility that there may be universes other than our own that possess widely different structures from "our own universe." Should we not consider seriously the possibility of the existence of such multiple universes—of an ensemble of actual (not merely possible) universes—among which our own universe is only one?

However, even if it is more conservative to suppose that the universe is unique and that one may plausibly continue to use the guidance of the standard relativity theory in its application to the subject matter of cosmology (on the conviction that while there may be various possible cosmological models, they are all to be regarded as so many different proposals to describe the actually existing *unique* universe), this decision poses further unsettling questions. For the attempt to describe the universe as a unique whole by the application of laws whose very nature allows multiple applications to a great variety of localized physical systems—as is the case with the variety of applications of the field equations of the general theory of relativity—this raises questions concerning the soundness of making such an application to the subject matter that is of special interest to cosmology. For in standard applications of physical laws (especially those stated in differential form), one normally distinguishes "accidental, initial, boundary conditions" from those properties "essential" and invariant to all cases falling under the law. However, this distinction breaks down in dealing with the putatively unique physical system that the universe as a whole is thought to be. In considering the universe as a whole as a unique, all-inclusive physical system, can we continue to use the distinction between what is invariant or essential and what is accidental or a matter of special boundary conditions? In order to continue to fall back on the standard procedure of using the laws and principles of physics to describe the physical structure of the universe, would it not be more circumspect and defensible, therefore, to think of the universe as *a very large system* to which the laws are applied, rather than as an absolute, unique whole? Perhaps, then, the concept of the universe as a whole is not, after all, the well-defined concept it was initially claimed to be!

Even if one overcame the foregoing scruples and reservations, there is a final difficulty associated with reliance on general relativity as the basic conceptual or theoretical tool for making the universe as a whole physically intelligible. It is that, when so applied, the theory leads to a breakdown of its conceptual capacities when dealing with sufficiently strong gravitational fields. And this is the case when, in applying the theory, one seeks to understand, retrodictively, the physics holding for the point in the past when the expansion of the universe began. It leads to physical singularities in the models constructed with its aid: "These singularities limit the validity of our claim that general relativity provides us with a selfconsistent treatment of the whole universe."[5]

[5] Sciama, "The Universe as a Whole," 19.

In the light of the foregoing reservations to his initial "grandiose claim," Sciama makes the following intriguing statement by way of conclusion to his discussion: "We conclude that both theoretically and observationally the universe (*probably*) exists" (my italics).[6] Confronted with this apparently more modest claim, we are driven to ask: Is it possible, then, that the universe *doesn't exist*? Prodded by Sciama's remarks, along with other incentives, we come back to the question with which we started: Does the universe exist? Let us turn to see what progress, if any, we can make by way of reply.

In current cosmology, the expression "universe" is used in two principally different yet related contexts. A common way of labeling these different contexts is to distinguish the special interests of observational cosmology and theoretical cosmology. The first use of the term "universe" is connected with the kind and scope of results obtained by the use of the tools of the observational astronomer in exploring the most comprehensive domain accessible to his instruments. The other is connected with the mathematical physicist's interest in constructing a model of the universe as a whole. This is accomplished by applying the conceptual resources of available physical theory to describe the most inclusive physical system allowed by those resources. While each type of specialist contributes in an important way to carrying out the complex overall project of cosmology, there are major differences in orientation, methodology, and operative standards of evaluation for judging the results obtained by each. It is convenient to use the expression "the observable universe" to refer to the limited domain of phenomena actually explored by available instruments at a particular stage of inquiry, and the expression "the universe as a whole" as the target of interest for the cosmologist operating on the level of physical theory.

Let us take advantage of the foregoing distinction. Instead of seeking a direct answer to the question "Does the universe exist?" let us reformulate our question into two separate questions: (1)

[6] Sciama, "The Universe as a Whole," 20.

Does the observable universe exist? and (2) Does the universe as a whole exist?

THE OBSERVABLE UNIVERSE

For the observational astronomer-cosmologist, the principal interest is to obtain reliable observational data concerning the variety of objects, events, and processes lying within the most comprehensive spatial and temporal domain accessible to available instruments. As an empirically grounded science, cosmology is stimulated to its inquiries by already accumulated observational data and ultimately returns for corroboration of predictions derived from its theories to the observational information obtained by means of optical or other types of telescopes and other instruments. Taken together, these instruments furnish detailed data about objects and processes located within a volume of space stretching outward from our station here on Earth to the most remote, accessible frontiers of the observable domain. As such research continues to explore the depths of the heavens, a fund of information is built up that specifies the relative individual locations, spatial distribution, sizes, patterns of motion, spectra, luminosities, and so on of the objects and physical systems encountered. The fund of information is, of course, not a matter of "pure observational data," for if by "pure" is meant "devoid of, or independent of" any conceptual interpretation furnished by physical theory, there are no such data. Observation and theory in cosmology, as in any empirical science, are inextricably intertwined. Thus theory will furnish the concepts for interpreting (or reinterpreting) already accumulated or newly acquired observational data, and in many cases give clues about where to look for and possibly discover hitherto unrecognized objects or occurrences. While acknowledging the important and omnipresent role of theory in the work of the observational astronomer-cosmologist, the use of the term "observational" is still warranted in order to give emphasis to the kinds of research projects the astronomer would normally pursue, and the types of special tools he or she would use. Progress in cosmology on an observational level can thus be roughly correlated with the degree of increasing adequacy in the quantity and character of the observational data thereby amassed.

For the actual use of the expression "observable universe" (or close cognates), a number of examples can be given. Consider the following account (written more than fifty years ago) given by Edwin Hubble, the great pioneer in contemporary observational cosmology.

> From our position somewhere within the [solar] system, we look out through the swarm of stars, past the borders, into the universe beyond. . . . The universe is empty, for the most part, but here and there, separated by immense intervals, we find other stellar systems, comparable with our own. . . . They are scattered through space as far as telescopes can penetrate. We see a few that appear large and bright. These are the nearer nebulae. Then we find them smaller and fainter, in constantly increasing numbers, and we know that we are reaching out into space, farther and ever farther, until, with the faintest nebulae that can be detected with the greatest telescope, we arrive at the frontiers of the known universe. This last horizon defines the observable region of space.[7]

In the above excerpt, as in his other writings, Hubble uses the expression "observable region" rather than "observable universe." Despite this, what he has to say is a clear and historically important example of the use of the alternative expression "observable universe." Moreover, although recent observational cosmology has advanced a good deal beyond Hubble's description of the "realm of nebulae," his account still serves as a valuable paradigm of the use of the concept "observable universe." Any currently favored description of the observable universe displays an

[7] Edwin Hubble, *The Realm of the Nebulae* (New Haven: Yale University Press, 1936), 20f.

obvious strong degree of family resemblance to the description Hubble gives. There is every reason to expect, too, that as astronomical inquiry continues into the future, further descriptions of the observable universe, as extensions and refinements upon those currently favored, will be forthcoming.

No seriously considered cosmological model in current scientific cosmology takes the observable universe to be coextensive with what it considers to be the universe as a whole, or even coextensive with an increasingly *larger* observable domain that lies beyond the bounds of what is observed at the present time. However rich and increasingly detailed the survey of the observable universe may be, current cosmology recognizes various limitations and horizons that bound it. For example, there is a general consensus that insofar as the observable region is identified with the currently explored domain of galaxies and clusters of galaxies, this does not exhaust the more inclusive domain of such systems that would be observed with more powerful instruments stretching into deeper reaches of space. Moreover, there are undoubtedly many other entities or types of phenomena that would be brought into view if observations were to continue over very long stretches of time.

Of the limitations or horizons that define the bounds of the observable universe, some are fixed, others movable. Some are of a technological nature having to do with the limitations in number and sensitivity of available astronomical instruments. Even with the combined use of present-day optical, radio, X-ray, and infrared telescopes (whether Earth-bound or satellite-mounted), definite bounds in sensitivity and range are encountered, although it may also be expected that new bounds would reappear whatever the degree of any marked improvement in data-gathering resources and new types of instrumental probes may be.

Other types of constraining conditions (beyond the primarily instrumental) that affect any description of the extent of the observable universe are fixed unalterably if one makes use of certain laws of physics or the currently accepted account of the overall character of the evolutionary development of the universe.

In this general category, an important type of restriction affecting the range of data used to characterize the observable universe is due to the maximum finite velocity of light. Thus even according to a simplified and admittedly unrealistic model of a static and Euclidean universe, an observer attached to our galaxy occupies the center of an observable region whose spatial extent is defined by the surface of a three-dimensional sphere. This surface divides the entire domain of objects into two subdomains: those that fall within the bounds of the surface, and so define the observable universe, and those that lie outside. Only those objects and events whose existence and occurrence fall within the sphere set by the time it takes for information to reach us here on Earth are observable at a given time. The observable region does not extend beyond the distance it takes light to reach the observer from the most distant galaxies, while other objects will be unobservable since the light coming from them will not have had time to reach the observer at the moment of observation. In order to obtain information conveyed by electromagnetic radiation of what lies beyond this sphere, one would have to wait for light to catch up with the relatively fixed situation of the observer and bring news about what belongs to a space-time region beyond the limits of the then-observable region. While at a given moment of time this type of horizon—known as "the particle horizon"—is fixed for an observer situated at a particular spatial location, the horizon shifts with the advance of time and to this extent it is movable, since objects hitherto lying outside the range of observability now come into view. Additional adjustments to determine the horizon of the observable universe beyond those set by the finite velocity of light are required due to the expansion of the observable universe as evidenced by the systematic redshift of the galaxies.

Still other types of limitation are enforced by the evolutionary development of the universe as currently known. Microwave background radiation, observationally established by Penzias and

Wilson in 1965, has expanded the horizon of the observable universe to the pregalactic era—to the stage in the remote past before galaxies themselves were formed—when photons were liberated from their coupling with matter. As a carrier of information, electromagnetic energy in the form of microwave background radiation became available only roughly 100,000 years after the Big Bang. Thus any occurrences before this time are not observable by this means. This is known as "the photon horizon" and should be distinguished from the horizon set by the finite velocity of light. It is another example of the observer's dependence on specific types of information-bearing messengers over which the observer has no control.

Many other examples can be cited to support the general conclusion that what is encompassed under the heading "the observable universe" is observationally bounded in various ways. In short, the term "observable universe," as used in current cosmology, stands for the limited domain of cosmologically relevant objects and processes accessible to observational identification and exploration at a particular stage of inquiry.

The foregoing brief synopsis of some of the main features of the observable universe recognized in current cosmology leads us next to consider the way in which we should regard the use of the expression "the observable universe" from the vantage point of philosophy of language. Then we can see what light such use might shed on the question of determining what is involved in affirming the *existence* or *intelligibility* of the observable universe in the context of scientific inquiry.

In examining the expression "exists" in a sentence of the general form "x exists," a basic distinction is required between questions of *meaning* and questions of *truth*. On the level of meaning, to say "x exists" may be understood as having to do with specifying criteria or standards that would have to be satisfied if a statement of the form "x exists" is to be judged as true or false. On the other hand, given some accepted set of criteria for specifying the meaning of "exists," the question may still arise whether some or all of these criteria are satisfied in a particular situation.

This is a question of *truth* (or falsity). And here one would normally offer specific evidence of a relevant sort, depending on the context or type of "reality" being considered—for example, reports of observations and measurements in the case of a subject matter investigated by one of the empirical sciences. If themselves accepted as true, such evidential statements are used to support the general conclusion that for some particular value for the variable *x*, in "*x* exists," the resulting statement is true. With respect to such questions of truth, relevant distinctions in degrees of evidential support would normally be made. For example, to say that the Andromeda galaxy or the recently detected supernova explosion (Supernova 1987A) *exists*—that certain well-confirmed statements about each is accepted as true—has a different degree of evidential support attached to it, than, say, the truth of an assertion that there is a black hole in some particular galaxy (about which there may be disagreement among experts), or the classification used in describing a recently reported bright infra-red radiation as belonging to a hitherto unobserved type of source estimated to be as much as 17 billion years old.

The use of observation, as publicly carried out and confirmed, is a commonly employed criterion in everyday experience for establishing the existence of certain types of object. If one says "The Moon exists," it is tantamount to saying—while pointing to a certain demarcated, brightly illuminated portion of the sky—"Look and see for yourself," or "Countless persons all over the Earth and throughout history have observed this object." Indeed, nowadays one is not even restricted to making ordinary visual observations from our vantage point on Earth, but one can even journey to the Moon and traverse it, or use various sophisticated instruments to scan, identify, and measure its various features.

However, what belongs under the heading of "observation" may involve many complex factors and considerations, both in the case of the Moon and other types of commonly identifed objects, and especially in the case of processes and entities recognized primarily on sophisticated levels of scientific inquiry. The term "observation" or "observational data" accordingly covers a good deal more than "what meets the eye." To supplement the rudimentary exercise of perceptual or measuring facilities, the statement "such-and-such exists" amounts to saying "The statement is true, insofar as it is accepted by a community of qualified persons using a commonly shared set of criteria for making this appraisal with respect to the entity or entities under consideration, as these are described in the language employed by those making this judgment." For example, does one *observe* the weak gravitational field of the Moon? When we saw Armstrong "bounce around" as he "walked" on the Moon, did we also "see" the weak gravitational field of the Moon that (according to current science) interprets and explains what we saw? Many would be inclined to answer in the affirmative.[8]

Examples such as the foregoing remind us that the appeal to observation as a method for establishing belief in the existence of something always carries with it linguistic and conceptual means for making what we observe intelligible in some way. Such conceptual components in observation encompass the use of various types of language schemes, whether natural or technical. The description and explanation of observable entities is, in the case of the advanced sciences, a question of bringing to bear concepts whose grammar is set out in a technical language. To give due attention to this conceptual component leaves open the matter of specifying, for a given scheme of thought adopted by a commu-

---

[8] Consider the following comparable situation: Do modern high-powered accelerators make possible the observation of genuinely existing electrons, photons, quarks, and neutrinos as these are described by the theoretical physicist? Some would have no hesitancy in answering in the affirmative, as in the following statement by a recent contributor to the theory of quarks: "QCD [quantum chromodynamics]—as the modern asymptotically free theory of the strong interaction is now called—has gone from success to success, and it is now universally recognized to be *the* theory of the strong interaction. At today's accelerators, quarks and gluons leave their signature in an extremely legible form—you can practically *see* them in pictures of the stuff emerging from ultra high-energy collisions, indirectly but quite clearly. They leave narrow trails of particles in their wake, like the plume a jet plane writes across the sky." See Frank Wilczek and Betsy Devine, *Longing for the Harmonies* (New York: W. W. Norton, 1988), 216.

nity of competent judges, the distinctive set of criteria to be used in appraising a judgment as true or false when the claim is made that it is based on observation. We need to consider not only cases in which there is substantial agreement, but also the areas of controversy and difference of opinion at a particular stage of inquiry. These differences typically arise not only with respect to what is directly observable or measurable, but with respect to the conceptual tools to be applied in rendering intelligible what is observed. Decisions to accept physical theory clearly affect the appeal to observation as a method for establishing both the existence and the intelligibility of what is said to exist.

If the foregoing considerations apply when we deal with the existence (in the sense of the truth claims) concerning an observable object such as the Moon, we must expect that these types of consideration are also appropriate when we consider the existence and intelligibility of the observable universe. Let us adopt Hubble's term, for the moment, and think of the observable universe as a space-time "region" filled with all sorts of astronomical and physical processes, events, and objects. When we turn to the astronomer's and cosmologist's enumeration and description of the contents and kinds of processes found in this region, it is obvious that their accounts make use, at various points, of the conceptual resources of physical theory—for example, in interpreting the observed redshifts in the spectra of galaxies as being indicative of the expansion of the universe, or in explaining intense X-ray radiations as originating in the presence of neutron stars or black holes. Indeed, more generally, the sentences comprising an account of the observable universe are of various types: (1) descriptive sentences (factual statements) reporting actual perceptions, observations, and measurements (e.g., the galaxy classified as M33 is a spiral galaxy); (2) ostensive definitions and other types of grammatical rules (e.g., "redshift is a displacement of lines in a spectrogram toward the red end of the spectrum, obtained from certain astronomical sources, as compared with standard laboratory sources"); (3) mathematical and logical rules of calculation and inference (e.g., the differential calculus, Riemannian geometry, etc.); (4) equations summing up phenomenological laws (e.g., Hubble's law stating a linear correlation between the distance of a galaxy and its redshift); and (5) sentences conveying the basic ideas of underlying analogies and principles associated with one or another cosmological model or particular branch of physics (e.g., relativistic cosmology, quantum theory, particle physics). Reports of observation rest on (1) the data obtained from various instruments for observation and measurement; and (2) a fund of ostensive definitions or other grammatical rules that explains the meaning of expressions used in the course of setting out the observational data. Of course, neither the instruments in their manipulation nor the ostensive definitions and other grammatical rules themselves yield statements that can be appraised with respect to truth or falsity. In the case of observing or measuring instruments, the appropriate criteria of evaluation have to do with such matters as reliability and efficiency, whereas in the case of grammatical rules that explain the meaning of various technical expressions, they deal with such matters as clarity and consistency. However, none of these criteria is the same as those appealed to in judging the truth or falsity of statements reporting on or describing what is found through observation. From time to time, even certain items in the accumulated storehouse of previously accepted observational findings may undergo reconsideration and be reclassified, redescribed, or improved with respect to the accuracy of measured results. And, of course, with continuing inquiry, new additions to the fund of confirmed observational data will constitute the basis for making changes in how one explicates in detail what belongs to the observable universe. In short, the term "observable universe" has no fixed and constant referent. Accordingly, it is important to consider the *truth value* of various *statements* that belong to the *description* of the "region." If the expression "the observable universe" serves, for certain purposes, as a proxy for a series of sentences containing factual statements, then one can raise the question of the truth or falsity of the latter. Since the description of every observed object or system of astronomical objects and occurrences is also encased in and accompanied by descriptive terms that depend on linkages to conceptual schemes exhibiting different amounts of controversy or degrees of critical acceptance among competent investigators, it is obvious that what is called "observational data" is not the uniform and unqualified thing it might seem to be, and therefore the observable universe reported on by the "observational data" is a "theory-laden" term. The foregoing brief list of reminders of the complexity of the components that we must take into account in characterizing the observable universe at any stage of inquiry on the basis of so-called observational data should make it obvious that there is no single, fixed referent for the expression "the observable universe." We should be hard put to point, ostensively, to an object that could serve as the referent of this expression, and about which we can say "It exists."

If we accept the foregoing, what response should we make to the question, "Does the observable universe exist?" The answer cannot be a simple "yes" or "no." For not only are there different component elements that belong to the explication of what is encompassed under the expression "observable universe," but there are also different ways in which we might give sense to the expressions "exist" or "is real." Hence, by stressing different aspects of "observable universe" and different senses of "exist" in formulating the question, "Does the observable universe exist?" we should obtain a mix of "yes" and "no" answers. Say, for example, that our standard for determining if something exists is whether it can be "observed" (where the latter term is used in a relatively unanalyzed way). Then, if we gather together all statements about those objects, groups of objects, events, and processes—particularly those considered of relevance on a cosmic scale of spatial and temporal magnitude—for which astronomers have obtained confirming observational evidence; and if, moreover, we mean by "the observable universe" the rough totality of such data and accepted true statements, then our simple, rough answer might be "yes." However, since there are differences in the reliability, amount of consensus, and accuracy of the observational data on which such a response relies, we should attach different degrees of affirmation to these different items. Taking all this into account, along with the changing character and shifts in judgment brought by continuing research and discussion, we may qualify any initially simple, rough, affirmative answer to our question, when our principal interest is in examining the use of the expressions "observable universe," "exist," and "intelligible" in the context of scientific inquiry.

COSMOLOGICAL MODELS

The answer to the question whether the observable universe is to be identified with what may be conceived to be the universe as a whole is not found by appealing to observable data. It is not the function of astronomical observation per se to determine whether any synoptic survey of available data coincides in its range with what, on a conceptual level, is pictured to be the universe as a whole. This decision is made only in the light of the adoption of some model that specifies how the universe as a whole is to be conceived. Even more importantly, this decision rests at bottom on a philosophical view as to the epistemological role played by such cosmological models. It is to a consideration of this crucial topic that we turn next; here, we will focus our attention on how to answer the question, "Does the universe as a whole exist?"

As we have seen, the totality of objects, subsystems, processes, and events comprising the observable universe—insofar as these are known at the present time—is believed to be only a portion of some more inclusive system. It follows that whatever the different types of limits to the observable region may be, the only way to depict the composition and structure of a more inclusive system is conceptually to construct a model of what it may be thought to be. Indeed, a common way of describing the interest of theoretical cosmology is to say that it takes as its subject matter not simply a *more* inclusive system within which the observable universe is situated and by which it is encompassed, but rather the *most comprehensive* system of all—the single, integrated totality of physical objects and processes. According to this common way of thinking, what distinguishes the special concern of a cosmological model from other types of physical theories is that by its means one seeks to gain an understanding of this single, all-inclusive physical system: *the universe as a whole.*

In carrying out this type of project, cosmologists appeal to various resources, clues, and guides. These include analogies with less comprehensive physical systems, concepts and models of a fundamentally mathematical (e.g., geometrical) sort, statistical sampling principles, equations and concepts connected with widely used physical laws and theories, and so-called cosmological principles especially devised to apply only to the universe as a whole. It is normally expected that to the extent they are able to achieve their objective, cosmologists will not only render the maximally inclusive physical system itself intelligible, but will thereby also achieve a basic understanding of the phenomena in the relatively restricted domain of the observable universe.

We may take a few sentences from Einstein's description of his own first efforts in this direction as a paradigm of this conception of the goal of theoretical cosmology. In the section entitled "Considerations on the Universe as a Whole," taken from his book *Relativity: The Special and General Theory*, Einstein sketches the main ideas of his model of a spatially finite, unbounded universe:

> If we ponder over the question as to how the universe, considered as a whole, is to be regarded, the first answer that suggests itself is surely this: As regards space (and time) the universe is infinite. . . . But speculations on the structure of the universe also move in quite another direction. The development of non-Euclidean geometry led to the recognition of the fact, that we can cast doubt on the *infiniteness* of our space without coming into conflict with the laws of thought or with experience. . . . According to the general theory of relativity, the geometrical properties of space are not independent, but they are determined by matter. Thus we can draw conclusions about the geometrical structure of

the universe only if we base our considerations on the state of matter as being something that is known. We know from experience that, for a suitably chosen co-ordinate system, the velocities of stars are small as compared with the velocity of transmission of light. We can thus as a rough approximation arrive at a conclusion as to the nature of the universe as a whole, if we treat the matter as being at rest.[9]

In his use of the concepts and principles of the theory of general relativity to describe the universe as a whole, Einstein engaged in a venture of far wider scope of application for that theory than the earlier, highly successful use of its equations to describe the gravitational field of our local solar system. With the new venture in theoretical cosmology, Einstein opened a field of inquiry that came to be known as "relativistic cosmology." His own first efforts in this area consisted in the construction of a model of a static, spatially finite, and unbounded universe. The need to develop nonstatic models was shortly thereafter recognized, especially following upon Edwin Hubble's epoch-making observational discoveries (toward the end of the 1920s) of the systematic redshifts of the galaxies. These data suggested the existence of the phenomenon known as "the expansion of the universe." With the discovery of the Hubble law of the redshifts of extragalactic nebulae, cosmological models were developed that no longer adhered to the idea that the universe is static, when considered on a large scale and from a temporal point of view. In the course of developing such nonstatic models, Einstein's original leading idea of using a geometric interpretation for gravitation was retained by those who fashioned cosmological models based on the field equations of general relativity. When applied for cosmolog-

[9] Albert Einstein, *Relativity: The Special and General Theory*, trans. R. W. Lawson (London: Methuen, 1920; reprinted, New York: Peter Smith), part 3. The excerpt quoted is also in Milton K. Munitz, ed., *Theories of the Universe* (New York: Free Press, 1957), 275–279. Einstein's original paper, on which this summary is based, is translated as "Cosmological Considerations on the General Theory of Relativity" and appears in H. A. Lorentz et al., *The Principle of Relativity* (New York: Dover, n.d.).

ical purposes, these equations allowed not only the use of uniform spaces of positive, negative, or zero curvature to represent the observationally supported data of the overall uniform spatial distribution of the galaxies, but different patterns of temporal development for the space of the universe as a whole: those that are ever expanding, oscillating, or contracting. Different models belonging to relativistic cosmology, making use of these possible options, were accordingly constructed in the course of the next several decades, and applied to the astronomer's data that showed the galaxies to have an overall uniform spatial distribution and an overall pattern of mutual recession. To this increasingly active field of relativistic model building, other investigators—among them, Alexander Friedmann, H. P. Robertson, Willem de Sitter, Georges Lemaître, and John Wheeler—made important contributions.[10]

Subsequent developments of theoretical cosmology, however, have not only taken into account more recent observational data, but have encouraged the use of other, more recent advances in mathematical physics, particularly various forms of quantum theory and particle physics. Their contributions involve going beyond the earlier general reliance on the geometric orientation of general relativity theory. These new conceptual resources have yielded important results in understanding the physical mechanisms at work at different stages of the evolutionary development of the universe. Among currently much discussed cosmological models are "the standard Hot Big Bang model," "the inflationary universe," and "the Hawking universe." These models, along with a variety of others, form a wide resemblance class with respect to explaining what it means to say that a cosmological model is devoted to describing the universe as a whole.

A dominantly philosophical interest in cosmological models, as distinguished from a purely technical interest in examining their internal details, is concerned with arriving at a considered

[10] For an account of these, see J. D. North, *The Measure of the Universe: A History of Modern Cosmology* (Oxford: Clarendon Press, 1965), chaps. 4–6.

view concerning their general epistemological and ontological worth. This latter type of interest can be illustrated by the following questions: When cosmological models are said to describe the universe as a whole, is this an essential or is it a dispensable concept for understanding the goals and accomplishments of cosmology? If we do employ the concept of the universe as a whole, must we think of this expression as having a referential role—as a name for or description of an entity that exists independently and possesses its own inherent structure apart from all inquiry, thought, and language? If we take this concept as indispensable, does the expression "the universe as a whole" refer to an entity that is unobservable? Might it not be preferable to interpret cosmology as interested in giving an account of a *larger physical system* to which the observable universe belongs, without presupposing the existence of an independently existing *largest system*? Is there any difference, pragmatically, between these contrasting interpretations in judging the values of the outcome of any cosmological venture?

One way of bringing the above questions into a single focus is to examine the question, "Does the universe as a whole exist?" In this discussion, we will examine the roles performed by a cosmological model in relation to the observable universe. Our primary interest will be to see to what extent (or in what sense or senses) we may think of the cosmological model as being *true*. In particular, our analysis will enable us to see the difficulties encountered by using the expression "the universe as a whole" as a name (a singular referring expression) for an "object" of the most inclusive sort.[11]

In general, a cosmological model may be considered from two

---

[11] In his exposition of the arguments for the existence of God, as given by Thomas Aquinas, Peter Geach remarks: "I shall argue that what is in fact essential to the 'Five Ways' is something tantamount to treating the world as a great big object. (It is after all natural to us to so regard the world—'Heaven and Earth', as it is called in the Old Testament—as the upper limit of the series: Earth, solar system, galaxy, cluster of galaxies, . . .)." See G.E.M. Anscombe and P. T. Geach, *Three Philosophers* (Oxford: Basil Blackwell, 1961), 112.

points of view: (1) what it says: its meaning; and (2) its truth value: how good is it when compared to other accounts in saying "how things are," "what the facts are." This broad division of components in all cosmological models may accordingly be divided into two main groups: (1) those that belong, in the Wittgensteinian sense, to grammatical rules; and (2) the application of these rules for purposes of explanation, description, and prediction. Both aspects are necessary in order to have a reasonably complete, adequately functioning conceptual scheme.

Within the class of the grammatical rules belonging to a cosmological model, we can distinguish the following major subgroups.

The Leading Idea

One subgroup is the feature I shall refer to as the model's "leading idea." Within the group of grammatical rules of a cosmological model, the leading idea occupies pride of place: it is the most important means for distinguishing a cosmological model from others, and marks its innovative character when compared to other conceptual schemes. It is frequently recognized by the use of the originator's name, for example, that of Einstein, de Sitter, or Hawking; or by a shorthand expression, for example, "Big Bang," "inflationary," "steady state."

The project of determining the meaning of a leading idea is comparable to that of coming to understand any other convention, stipulation, or linguistic rule. An explanation of its meaning seeks to establish comprehension and competence in its use by those to whom the explanations are directed. Such comprehension and competence are necessary preliminaries to and conditions for subsequent applications of the new conceptual tool. When explaining and understanding the leading idea's meaning, it is inappropriate and irrelevant to raise questions with respect to its truth or falsity. These evaluative judgments come later, when the idea is applied for purposes of factual description, prediction, or causal explanation. Let us consider some prominent examples of leading ideas in recent cosmology.

1. EINSTEIN'S GEOMETRIC APPROACH TO GRAVITATION

A paradigm of a leading idea in cosmology is Einstein's adoption of his own, more general, revolutionary proposal to treat gravitation in terms of the geometric property of curvature. The field equations of the general theory of relativity, already formulated in 1915, established a precise mathematically expressed connection between the curvature of a gravitational field and the distribution of the density of mass-energy in the field. It was the application of this conception of gravitation to the distinctive physical system of the universe as a whole that constituted Einstein's leading idea in cosmology, an idea he worked out in the paper he published on this subject in 1917. He undertook to describe the geometric space-time curvature associated with the mass-energy distribution determining the gravitational field belonging to the largest of all physical systems. Einstein proposed that the overall spatial structure of the universe as a whole is uniform, finite, and unbounded—in short, positively curved. In order to yield what Einstein assumed to be a necessary property of the universe, that it show no overall temporal pattern of change, Einstein modified the original equations of general relativity by introducing a cosmological constant, representing a cosmical repulsion factor, operative over very large volumes of space, to balance the attraction of gravitation. (He later called the introduction of this cosmological constant "the greatest blunder of my life.")

2. MILNE'S KINEMATIC RELATIVITY

A different type of cosmological model from those based on the use of the general theory of relativity was suggested in the 1930s by British cosmologist E. A. Milne. He too sought to incorporate the notion of the universe as undergoing expansion, but without employing the notion of expanding space or the underlying dynamical concepts of the general theory of relativity. The leading idea of his own model of the expanding universe was based entirely on kinematic considerations. For Milne,

> The principle of relativity is in effect used in a new way, a way which is almost independent of observational verification; it is employed in the self-evident form that two observers, who stand in equivalent relations to the system and who agree to combine their observations (to yield coordinates) according to the same rules, will describe the behaviour of any particle by the same functions of these coordinates. . . . The leading idea in our work is not that of transformations of *coordinates* but of transformations from *observer to 'equivalent' observer*, where the word equivalent will be strictly defined in terms of observations and tests which the observers can actually carry out.[12]

3. THE STEADY STATE MODEL

Another cosmological model that received wide attention for about two decades beginning in the late 1940s was the steady state ("continuous creation") model associated with the names of Fred Hoyle, Hermann Bondi, and Thomas Gold. In order to avoid what was for these authors the philosophically "unwelcome" idea that the universe had a beginning in time, as this was inferred by then current evolutionary models of the expanding universe, appeal was made to two distinctive leading ideas. One went by the name "the Perfect Cosmological Principle," according to which not only are all cosmological facts fundamentally the same when considered *spatially* from any point in the universe, but a general uniformity of all cosmological phenomena also prevails at any

[12] E. A. Milne, *Relativity, Gravitation, and World-Structure* (Oxford: Clarendon Press, 1935), 4–5; cf. Munitz, *Space, Time, and Creation: Philosophical Aspects of Scientific Cosmology* (Glencoe, Ill.: Free Press, 1957; 2d ed., New York: Dover, 1981), chap. 6.

time in the infinite past or infinite future of the universe. Insofar as one adheres to a belief in the standard law of the conservation of mass-energy, together with the reliance on the observed expansion of the universe, this would result over a period of time in an average decrease in the density of the universe. To avoid the latter consequence, and in order to satisfy the Perfect Cosmological Principle, the steady state model postulates a continuous creation of matter at the statistically steady rate of one hydrogen atom per cubic meter of volume every 5 billion years—a creation rate that would hold in all epochs and throughout space. If there were such a creation rate, the newly created matter would eventually form composite material structures of the dimensions of galaxies that would thereby replace the receding older galaxies moving beyond the horizon of the observable universe. The continuous creation of matter would accordingly maintain the universe in a steady state.[13]

4. THE HOT BIG BANG

A major observational discovery, in 1965, of the cosmic microwave background radiation led to the abandonment of the steady state model. It pointed to the need of accepting an evolutionary model of the universe: a universe having a finite beginning in the past and manifesting a pattern of change over the course of time. In addition to the inference, on the basis of the geometrically oriented relativistic models, that there was a point ($t = 0$) in the finite past, marked by an infinite density and infinite curvature, at which the universe began its expansion, an explanation of the physical conditions that prevailed at the original production of the microwave radiation yielded the retrodiction to a *"Hot* Big Bang" origin of the universe.

The recent, rapidly accumulating insights of quantum field

[13] Cf. H. Bondi and T. Gold, *Mon. Not. Roy. Astr. Soc.* 108 (1948); F. Hoyle, *Mon. Not. Roy. Astr. Soc.* 108 (1948); F. Hoyle, *Mon. Not. Roy. Astr. Soc.* 109 (1949); H. Bondi, *Cosmology* (Cambridge, Eng.: Cambridge University Press, 1952), chap. 12; Munitz, *Space, Time, and Creation*, chap. 8.

theories, as well as other contributions to elementary particle physics, have made possible an enriched understanding of the physics involved in the evolutionary development of the universe over and above the insights afforded by a purely geometric account of its stages.[14] These contributions, representing the convergence of interest of particle physics and cosmology, concerned especially the early period ("the first three minutes") and very early period (as close as up to 10^{-43} sec) following the Hot Big Bang. Especially important in their contributions to this standard Hot Big Bang model of the universe were ideas having to do with energy and temperature conditions under which the various fundamental forces—gravitational, electromagnetic, and weak and strong nuclear forces—and their associated particles existed at different stages. At extremely high temperatures, particular combinations of these forces existed in states of unification or symmetry. As a result of the expansion of the universe and accompanying drops in temperature, particular stages of symmetry were followed by differentiation among some of these forces by a process known as "symmetry breaking." In short, by taking into account prevalent particles and forces present during particular epochs in the evolution of the universe, differences among these stages were discernible. The stages are identifiable according to the types of physical conditions that characterized the moments at which the symmetries either became "frozen" at certain levels or began their phase transitions to other levels. The working out of cosmological models that are able to take advantage of these rapidly accumulating insights of elementary particle physics is the focal point of current cosmology.

There are two examples of such recent models, each exploiting its own distinctive leading idea and each undertaking to solve different special problems. One is the inflationary model, to which

[14] For an account of these advances, see Edward W. Kolb, Michael S. Turner, David Lindley, Keith Olive, and David Seckel, eds., *Inner Space Outer Space: The Interface between Cosmology and Particle Physics* (Chicago and London: University of Chicago Press, 1986).

Alan Guth made early, important contributions, and the other is Stephen Hawking's recent effort to specify the wave function of the universe.

5. THE INFLATIONARY MODEL

Despite its great successes and plausibility, there were various problems connected with the standard Hot Big Bang model. Among these problems were those technically known as the "flatness" and "horizon" problems.[15] Guth and others proposed ways of overcoming both these problems. The leading idea was to conceive the universe as having undergone an exponentially increasing inflationary period of spatial expansion during a very brief period beginning at 10^{-35} second within the first second after the Big Bang. During this extremely short period of expansion, there occurred an enormous release of latent energies, consequent reheating, and radical phase transitions of various sorts.[16] By making use of such technical notions as "true vacuum," "false vacuum," "Higgs fields," "spontaneous symmetry breaking," and "negative pressure that can lead to a gravitational force that is effectively repulsive," the inflationary model describes the kinds of conditions in the very early universe that prevailed during its inflationary expansion.

This period of accelerated expansion is called the inflationary era, and it is the key element of the inflationary model of the universe. According to the model, the inflationary era continued for 10^{-32} second or longer, and during this period the diameter of the universe increased by a factor of 10^{50} or more. It is assumed that after this collossal expansion the transition to the broken symmetry phase finally took place. The energy density of the false vacuum was then released,

---

[15] For a brief account of these problems, see below, pp. 170–172.

[16] Cf. A. Guth and P. Steinhardt, "The Inflationary Universe," *Scientific American*, May 1984, 116–128; reprinted, Paul Davies, ed., *The New Physics* (Cambridge, Eng.: Cambridge University Press, 1989), 34–60. A. D. Linde, "The Inflationary Universe," *Rep. Prog. Phys.* 47 (1984): 925–986.

resulting in a tremendous amount of particle production. The region was reheated to a temperature of almost 10^{27} degrees [K]. (In the language of thermodynamics the energy released is called the latent heat; it is analogous to the energy released when water freezes.) From this point on the region would continue to expand and cool at the rate described by the standard big-bang model.[17]

6. HAWKING'S WAVE FUNCTION MODEL

A major feature of most cosmological models that trace back the finite past history of the universe to a Big Bang is to treat this event as a physical singularity, that is to say, as an occurrence whose physics is not understood. A physical singularity marks the breakdown of the conceptual resources of a theory. The situation, thus identified, will either have to be taken as an arbitrary initial condition or, if explainable, will have to await fresh, hitherto unavailable conceptual tools. Science generally, and cosmology in particular, cannot live contentedly with singularities. Another competent theory of wider scope and greater competence will be sought. It is this situation that has inspired a number of attempts in recent cosmology to explain the singularity called the Big Bang. Among those sharing in these attempts is Stephen Hawking. His basic strategy is to bring to bear newly devised approaches to quantum gravity in order to describe the physical situation out of which the universe arose. If successful, his effort would show how the beginning of the universe can be understood without needing to regard it as a singularity, or something whose explanation must be left to metaphysics or religion. Let Hawking describe these efforts:

> The real problem with spacetime having an edge or boundary at a singularity is that the laws of science do not determine the initial state of the universe at the singularity but only how it evolves thereafter. This problem would remain even if there were no singularity and time continued back

[17] Guth and Steinhardt, "The Inflationary Universe," 122.

indefinitely: the laws of science would not fix what the state of the universe was in the infinite past. In order to pick out one particular state for the universe from among the set of all possible states that are allowed by the laws, one has to supplement the laws by boundary conditions that say what the state of the universe was at an initial singularity or in the infinite past. . . .

In the classical general theory of relativity, which does not incorporate the uncertainty principle, the initial state of the universe is a point of infinite density. It is very difficult to define what the boundary conditions of the universe should be at such a singularity. However, when quantum mechanics is taken into account, there is the possibility that the singularity may be smeared out and that space and time together may form a closed four-dimensional surface without boundary or edge. This would mean that the universe was completely self-contained and did not require boundary conditions. One would not have to specify the state in the infinite past and there would not be any singularities at which the laws of physics would break down. One could say that the boundary conditions of the universe are that it has no boundary. . . .

What happened at the beginning of the expansion of the universe? Did spacetime have an edge at the Big Bang? The answer is that if the boundary conditions of the universe are that it has no boundary, time ceases to be well-defined in the very early universe just as the direction 'North' ceases to be well-defined at the North Pole of the Earth.[18]

[18] S. W. Hawking, "The Edge of Spacetime," in William J. Kaufmann, III, *Universe* (New York: W. H. Freeman, 1985), 567; cf. S. W. Hawking, "Quantum Cosmology," in Bryce S. DeWitt and Raymond Stora, *Relativity, Groups and Topology II*, Les Houches, Session 40, Course 4 (New York: Elsevier, 1984); S. W. Hawking, "The Quantum State of the Universe," *Nuclear Physics B* 239 (1984): 257–276; S. W. Hawking, *A Brief History of Time* (New York: Bantam Books, 1988); S. W. Hawking, "Quantum Cosmology," in S. W. Hawking and

So much for a brief sampling of some of the leading ideas that animate the most prominent cosmological models of the recent past. The originality, freshness, and innovative character of a leading idea is not arrived at through an inductive process of generalizing the common features of a mass of observational data. Sometimes the idea is arrived at by way of extending an established law or theory in a novel way, as was the case with Einstein's use of his own general theory of relativity, or Guth's use of certain well-known ideas of classical thermodynamics; sometimes the idea comes by inventing a special principle, as was the case with the adoption of the Perfect Cosmological Principle by those upholding the steady state theory; and sometimes it comes by borrowing from quantum field theories the idea of virtual particles present in a vacuum state, to describe the pre-Big Bang genesis of the primordial cosmic quantum particle out of which the entire universe later grew. All these leading ideas are the outcome of creative inspiration, novel ways of approaching the special area of cosmology.

Other Grammatical Rules

The leading idea, however, is not the only member of the group of grammatical rules employed in a cosmological model. The others are borrowed from their standard contexts of use. And although they, too, at one time were the products of innovative, creative thought, they will have achieved conventional, standardized, routine acceptance. To supplement its distinctive and novel leading idea, a cosmological model will normally make use of these accepted laws and theories of physics in order to yield predictions, explanations, and classifications with respect to observational data not already brought within the scope of the leading idea for these purposes. Further, there will be a host of mathematical rules of inference, either already standardly incorporated

W. Israel, eds., 300 *Years of Gravitation* (Cambridge, Eng.: Cambridge University Press, 1987), 631–651.

in physical theories or freshly borrowed from the "archives" of mathematics. These rules will be employed for performing various calculations and in judging the soundness of inferences. These too are grammatical rules to be explained, understood, and mastered. In addition to the foregoing grammatical rules, there is a vast, motley group of concepts, linguistic expressions, and principles of ordinary language, common sense, or of some favored world view that are also part of the grammar of a cosmological model.

Taking now the combination of the leading idea of a cosmological model and a variety of ancillary grammatical rules of the sort just mentioned, let us turn next to consider the typical uses to which this combination of ideas and rules will be put. Among the mutliple functions and possible accomplishments of a cosmological model, we may distinguish the following.

1. REDESCRIPTION OF OBSERVATIONAL DATA

One use of a cosmological model is to provide a conceptual scheme for reinterpreting certain already known observational facts: the new conceptual interpretation amounts to a redescription, a new way of looking at familiar observational data. This may win the gradual acceptance of cosmologists because it offers a more satisfactory, "illuminating" way of thinking than do conventional ways. A good example of this is the kind of interpretation now widely adopted for understanding Hubble's Law—the generalization that establishes a linear correlation between the distance of galaxies and their redshifts. A standard interpretation of a redshift phenomenon employed in conventional physics is to treat it as a sign of a Doppler-type effect in the sphere of electromagnetic behavior—an effect comparable to what is already familiar in the case of sound. On this standard Doppler interpretation, the recording of a redshift in the line spectra of light received from a distant galaxy is due to the relative motions in space of the emitting source of radiation and its receiver. On this interpretation, the redshift is evidence of the galaxy's motion of recession *through* space, relative to the position of the observer.

By contrast with this description, the interpretation offered by a cosmological model employing the leading idea of relativistic cosmology—that the space of the universe is expanding—is this. The redshift is not due to the recessional motion of a galaxy through space, but rather to the expansion *of* space. When understood geometrically, the expansion of space is linked to the increase in length of the radius of curvature, R, of cosmic space very much in the same way as the increase in the length of the radius of a three-dimensional sphere results in an increase not only in the volume of the sphere but also affects the increase in the mutual distances between fixed points on the two-dimensional surface. In the case of the universe, one is dealing with a system described as a four-dimensional space-time continuum, in which the three dimensions of space define a geometrically conceived "hypersurface." On this hypersurface, the galaxies are situated in a basically fixed way, that is, they do not have any marked individual *local* motions. Rather, their changes of distance with respect to each other are due to the changes in the area of the hypersurface itself.

Furthermore, the space of the universe is taken to be fundamentally uniform over very large regions. It will have an overall geometry chosen from one of the three available types of metric geometries: Euclidean, hyperbolic, or spherical. Let $R(t)$ represent the functional relation between R, the radius of the curvature of space, and t, the cosmic time; in a particular model, the radius of curvature R will be thought of as belonging to one of these uniform geometries. The selected radius of curvature will perform the role of a cosmological *scale factor*. Since R is a function of t, the change in R will represent a change in the scale factor over periods of cosmic time. Thus let R_o represent its value at the present stage of the evolution of the universe, and let R represent its value at some other time, say at some time in the past. Then the expansion of the universe may be represented, in geometric terms, as an increase of the length of R when one compares its present value, R_o, to its value at an earlier time. Among other results, an increase in this scale factor, marking the expansion of space, would also have an effect on the wavelengths of electromagnetic radiation emitted by galaxies. There will be a change in the wavelength of this radiation—its increase and displacement toward the red end of the spectrum—if one compares its value at the time of its emission and its value at the time of reception by human observers on Earth. Let the redshift be expressed as a ratio $\frac{\lambda_o - \lambda}{\lambda}$, where λ_o is the wavelength of the received radiation and λ is the wavelength of the same radiation at the time of its emission. Then, instead of interpreting the redshift of galaxies whose radiation is recorded by observers on Earth as marking a conventional Doppler effect due to the relative motion of these galaxies regarded as receding sources *through* space, one can reinterpret the same phenomenon as due to the change in the scale factor of the universe—a change in the length of the radius of curvature $\frac{R_o - R}{R}$ of cosmic space.

2. SOLUTION OF PROBLEMS

Another important role performed by cosmological models is the proposal of solutions to one or more serious problems not satisfactorily dealt with by standard, accepted ways of thinking. A clear example of this situation is the problem presented by the apparently unavoidable inference to a physical singularity called the Big Bang, whether in older geometrically oriented models of the expanding universe or in more recent versions of the Hot Big Bang theory. It is this situation that has inspired a number of attempts in recent cosmology to explain scientifically the "event" called the Big Bang, an event which is frequently interpreted as marking the so-called origin of the universe at $t = 0$. Among such attempts is Hawking's recent effort at formulating a model in quantum cosmology that would not require assigning initial boundary conditions to the universe.

Another clear example of this problem-solving role of a cosmological model is found in Guth's and others' search for a way of dealing with the flatness and horizon problems left unsolved by the received Hot Big Bang model—problems in addition to the existence of the singularity of the Big Bang itself. These fresh problems were brought to the fore with the discovery by Penzias and Wilson in 1965 of the isotropic character of the microwave background radiation.

The flatness problem arises from the following considerations. The type of uniform geometry (curvature) that the universe might have is any one of three basic types: (1) flat, infinite, Euclidean, with zero curvature; (2) infinite, open, hyperbolic, with negative curvature; (3) spherical (or elliptic), finite, with positive curvature. Which of these it can have, according to physical theory, is determined by the actual density of matter and energy, ρ, in relation to the critical density, ρ_c or as measured too, in principle, by the deceleration parameter, q_0. If $q_0 = \frac{1}{2}$, that is, if the actual density is equal to the critical density, then the universe's geometry has zero curvature; if the value of q_0 lies between zero and $\frac{1}{2}$, space is open, negatively curved, and hyperbolic; and if the value of q_0 is greater than $\frac{1}{2}$, space is spherical and finite. The actual density is remarkably close to the value of the critical density, with a value of q_0 equal to one-half to more than fifty decimal places, showing that the geometry of the universe is just barely flat and infinite; however, any slight shift in either direction could change it to one or the other of the two geometries. What accounts for the remarkable "fine tuning" of this situation? This is the "flatness" problem.

The horizon problem, briefly, is this. The 3°K temperature of the background microwave radiation is uniform across the sky to one part in 10,000. With a distance of roughly 40 billion light years separating opposite sides of the observable universe, and thus exceeding by far the horizon or range within which light or causal influences could have been transmitted at the time when this uniformity of blackbody temperature was established, how can one account for the existence, nevertheless, of such remarkable uniformity of temperature in the microwave background radiation? This is the "horizon" problem.

The inflationary model, proposed by Guth and later modified by him and others, offers ways of solving both problems.

3. PREDICTION OF NEW OBSERVABLE PHENOMENA

A third important function of cosmological models is to extend the known range and contents of the observable universe by predicting hitherto unobserved details or ranges of observable occurrences and objects. As with other scientific theories, the success of these predictions will form an important basis in an evaluation of the truth-yielding capacities of the theory. Other considerations aside, the continued failure of a theory in this respect will be a sufficiently strong ground for its eventual abandonment or major overhaul.

There may have been broad sympathies shared by many with the general philosophic motivations of the authors of the steady state theory in adopting the Perfect Cosmological Principle, thereby avoiding the "need" to posit a beginning to the universe. This dispensing with the idea of a beginning to the universe was made possible by introducing the notion of a continuous creation of elementary particles to balance the observed recession of the galaxies. But it was the ultimate failure of the steady state model to square with the observations predicted for the character of galaxies and other phenomena beyond the horizons of the then known observed universe that led to its downfall. Some early contrary evidence to that predicted by the steady state theory was offered by Martin Ryle in connection with counts of faint celestial radio sources. These observations showed that the number of such radio sources was much too large when compared to the numbers that would be compatible with the steady state theory. Moreover, such sources lying at very great distances, having very large redshifts (hence belonging to a period in the very remote past) showed properties that can be explained only by assuming an evolutionary development of the universe. Similar contrary evidence to the predictions of the steady state theory was later forthcoming from observations on quasars. The coup de grace, however, was delivered by the discovery of the $3°K$ microwave background cosmic radiation. It was this evidence that convinced the overwhelming majority of cosmologists that, contrary to steady state predictions, the universe has undergone an evolutionary development in which its early stages were enormously dense and hence far different from the subsequent stages of the universe, including the present, which have been marked by increasing dilution of density.[19]

Further support for the Hot Big Bang cosmological model has come from astronomically confirmed predictions of that model concerning the conditions for primordial nucleosynthesis that prevailed in the universe during the first 1,000 seconds after the Big Bang. This data has to do with the relative abundance of such light elements as helium-3, helium-4, deuterium, and lithium-7. Further empirical tests of the model are now being widely pursued concerning its predictions that there must be at most only a small finite number (three or four) of families of quarks and leptons, the elementary particles believed to underlie all physical entities.[20]

Does Cosmology Need the Concept of "The Universe as a Whole"?

The reader may think that the account I have given thus far of the multiple roles and functions of a cosmological model is seriously incomplete. The roles I have mentioned—(1) the descriptive reinterpetation of observational data in terms of the distinctive conceptual tools of a model, especially its "leading idea"; (2) the solving of specific problems left unsolved in some widely accepted model by suggesting causal mechanisms not previously thought of; and (3) the making of predictions concerning hitherto unobserved aspects of the observable universe that can, if verified, extend the observable range of the observable universe and

[19] Cf. Dennis Sciama, "Cosmology Before and After the Quasars," *Scientific American*, September 1967.

[20] Cf. David N. Schramm and Gary Steigman, "Particle Accelerators Test Cosmological Theory," *Scientific American*, January 1988, 66–72.

thereby serve as tests of the model—are all perfectly genuine and important. They do not include, however, what is the most important role of all: the description of the universe as a whole. Unless this were not only included in the range of applications of the conceptual resources (the grammatical rules) of a model, but given priority over all the others, we should be getting a highly distorted and incomplete account of what a cosmological model is for. It would be another case of *Hamlet* without Hamlet.

How shall we respond to this criticism? The way I propose to do so takes us to the heart of our present discussion: what to say by way of answer to the question, "Does the universe as a whole exist?" Is it the ultimate goal of cosmology to fashion a cosmological model that will give a true description of the properties and structure of this objectively existing entity?

At an earlier stage of the present account, I made a broad distinction between two major types of features in a typical cosmological model: (1) those that belong to the purely conceptual part, its "grammatical rules" of various sorts, including especially its leading idea; and (2) those that apply the conceptual resources to yield factual knowledge in the form of descriptions, causal explanations, and predictions. Roughly, the first of these parts concerns the *meaning* of the formulation of the cosmological model, which has to do with understanding its grammatical rules. The second part has to do with questions concerning the *truth* about the subject matter dealt with. Without abandoning this important distinction, I shall propose a simplifying device for dealing with the question at hand: if we should say that the crucial and main subject matter to which a cosmological model addresses itself is the *existence* of the universe as a whole and that its main goal is to *discover the inherent properties* of this entity. In order to deal with this question, I propose as a useful strategy that we bracket, for now, the distinction just made between the conceptual and factual parts of a model, and consider the entire model—consisting of both parts—as if it were a single, complex conceptual tool, a "supergrammatical rule." We should next consider how, if this supergrammatical rule is applied for the sake of yielding factual knowledge, we should think of the universe as a whole as its principal domain of application.

In order to take advantage of this simplifying device for dealing with our main question, we must examine the following questions: Insofar as we regard the universe as a whole as being the main domain of application of our supergrammatical rule, is it to be thought of as having its own real, independent existence? And is it the ultimate goal of cosmology to fashion a cosmological model that will give a true description of the properties and structure of this objectively existing entity?

In general, a model is made in two types of circumstances. In one, there is no present or past experience of the actual existence of that of which the model is to be made; in the other, the object or situation to be modeled already exists, a method is available for identifying, recalling, or displaying it, and one looks for an adequate way to depict it. A particle physicist's description of the properties of the graviton (the postulated, though not as yet experimentally verified, carrier of the gravitational force) is an example of the first situation, a cartographer's map of a portion of the Earth's surface is a familiar example of the second.

Does the construction, articulation, and application of a cosmological model fit either of the foregoing types of situations? If we say that the universe as a whole is the subject matter for a cosmological model, is it something not known to actually exist, but nevertheless such that if we had an adequate model, we would be in a better position to undertake to identify it and to claim to have some description of it? Or is it something already known to exist yet still awaiting adequate description and knowledge of its properties? Or, as a third possibility, should we reject both these alternatives and look for another way of thinking of the role of a cosmological model?

An important first step toward responding to these questions is to concentrate on the phrase "the universe as a whole" and examine what can be said for treating it as if it were a *name* for an *entity*, in some way already understood and open to description, even though the entity is only sought and not yet identified. We ask, first: "Should we treat the expression 'the universe as a whole' as a denoting phrase, the referent of which is something of whose existence we are assured?"

If one were to give an affirmative answer to this question, we would normally expect that the one who is prepared to give this answer is in possession of either of two plausible grounds for giving an affirmative answer: one based on *direct experience* of a public and reliable sort, the other based on *inference* in accordance with some accepted principle.

As to the first of these possibilities, let us ask whether we have any direct evidence of a public and reliable sort that the universe as a *whole* exists. In the case of other cases where we use the term "whole" in connection with some object or situation, we do have ordinary grounds of a public and reliable sort to uphold the claim that we do confront, observe, or can identify the entity as a whole. Thus, in contrast with our having only a partial glimpse of a painting when seeing it displayed on the wall of a museum, we say that we see the whole of it when it is seen under optimal conditions and in an unobstructed way. We use the term "whole" in this everyday sense when referring to persons, animals, plants, and artifacts of various sorts. This is not equivalent to saying with respect to any such readily identifiable whole that we lay claim to understanding it completely, or that we know all its aspects adequately. Yet in a perfectly straightforward way we say, "We have the whole thing before us," "We saw the whole thing happen," and so on.

Do we have any similar way of claiming that the universe as a whole is also a matter of direct experience? The answer must surely be in the negative. It is sufficient to recall our earlier discussion of the observable universe. We found there is wide agreement among cosmologists that the observable universe as identified at the present time is *not* all that exists or that might be further observable. Indeed, some cosmologists might wish to say with respect to this wider domain that, even though it exists, not all of it might in principle be observable. In any case, there is broad consensus that the observable region is only a portion of a *more inclusive* domain, although there is no available, direct observational evidence *at the present stage of inquiry* of this wider domain, let alone any direct observational evidence of what may be thought to be the widest and *most inclusive* domain called "the universe as a whole." If we are to entertain the notion of the universe as a whole, this can only be done via the conceptual means of a cosmological model and not by directly available observational means.

If then one does believe in the existence of something denoted by the phrase "the universe as a whole," can this factual belief be supported by good reasons of an *inferential* sort? There are, broadly, two kinds of reasons of an inferential sort that might be offered. One is of a supposedly inductive character, the other of the kind that appeals to fundamental principles of a world picture or metaphysics.

To the question "How shall we conceive of the universe as a whole?" some cosmologists might respond by saying that we can obtain a satisfactory conception by using the knowledge obtained from the observable region as a fair sample of the whole. Hubble advocated this approach. He writes:

> The observable region of space, our sample of the universe, is now defined, and a preliminary reconnaissance has been completed. . . . As long as our positive information was restricted to the stellar system alone, the observable region then available could not possibly be regarded as a fair sample. . . . But now we have explored a certain portion of that outer space. Our observable region has been suddenly enlarged a million million fold. . . . Let us, then, follow the principle of the uniformity of nature and accept the observable region as a fair sample of the universe.[21]

[21] Edwin Hubble, *Observational Approach to Cosmology* (Oxford: Clarendon Press, 1937), chap. 1, "The Observable Region as a Sample of the Universe," 1, 19.

In evaluating Hubble's claim, let us consider the appropriateness of taking the familiar situation of regarding a part of a whole as a sample from which one may infer the properties of the whole as our guide in understanding the relation between the observable region and what is assumed to be the universe as a whole. There are many different contexts and uses for the notion of a sample. There are samples of particular specific properties or qualities, for example, colors, sounds, tastes; samples of classes, populations; specimen examples or paradigms of types of object, occurrence, action, behavior; and so on. Among the uses of samples are the following: (1) To *explain the meaning* of names or technical terms. Thus, to explain the meaning of a color name, say "red," one might choose a piece of cloth whose color is red, and by pointing to it, say "This is red." The object so used is part of the grammatical rule that explains the use of the term "red." (2) An altogether different role for samples is to serve as tools for making *statistical inferences* to wider classes. A pollster may appeal to the views of a selected group of persons in order to predict the outcome of an election. (3) A third use of samples is for *normative* purposes, as standards or paradigms to be emulated, copied, exemplified, duplicated. A person in charge of equipping an exhibit case in a museum will select suitable specimens, for example, patterns of teeth in a type of shark; a master craftsman luthier will illustrate, for the benefit of his students and apprentices, how to shape the scroll of a violin. Of this wide variety of uses of the notion of sample, that which involves taking the features of some part of a whole as a *sample* for inferring the properties of the whole, is the one most relevant to the question we have posed: "Is the observable region a sample of the universe as a whole?" The question at the moment is not whether the observable region is a fair sample, or whether in answering the latter question we can rely on the Principle of the Uniformity of Nature, but whether we can use the part-whole relation as a model for inferring from the observable region, considered as a part, to the universe as a whole.

In standard examples of using parts as bases for inferring the properties of a whole, as, for example, in predicting how the entire class or the whole of a voting populaton will vote, one is assured of the existence of the whole, and seeks to infer some property of it on the basis of what one finds in the part or sample. And in the normal case, where there is reasonable assurance of the existence of the whole, it is an important and legitimate question whether the part one is examining is a fair or representative sample of the whole. But in the case of the cosmological situation, short of begging the question by presupposing as indubitable that the universe as a whole does exist, one cannot use the model of the part-whole relation in its standard form to infer from the observable region what the properties of the putative whole—the universe—is. The question of fairness of the sample cannot even be raised, much less the question whether one can place reliance on the highly dubious Principle of the Uniformity of Nature in assuring such fairness. For these kinds of question do not arise before one has some sound basis for presupposing that there does exist something to be denominated "the universe as a whole" whose properties one is trying to infer on the basis of the data called "a sample." One can, to be sure, use the properties of the observable region as a basis for constructing a cosmological model of what is thought to be the universe as a whole, but this by itself does not guarantee that there is any independently existing entity, object, or system to which the model could be applied for descriptive or explanatory purposes.

If we cannot take Hubble's sample technique as a way of inferring to the independent existence of the universe as a whole and as a way of finding out about its properties, can we explain the use of the expression "the universe as a whole" in other ways?

One standard technique for providing an explanation of a term is to give examples of its use. However, one cannot give examples of the *applications* of the expression "the universe as a whole." For if, as we are here assuming, the expression is being used to designate a *unique* entity, there cannot be a multiplicity of examples. The terminology of "examples" is, in this context, altogether inappropriate. We cannot explain its use by offering examples that would constitute applications of the use of this term in making *true* statements. Here, to avoid misunderstanding, let me make clear that I am in no way denying that there could be a use of examples of the use of the term "the universe as a whole" insofar as this occurs in the course of setting out a cosmological model. And this use, in this way, is a perfectly legitimate way of explaining the meaning of the expression "cosmological model." For indeed the term "cosmological model" is a resemblance class expression of which there are multiple examples, any one of which could be used as a paradigm for explaining the use of this expression, and it is in these models that one does find the use of the expression "the universe as a whole." But of course to set out the meaning of the term "cosmological model," even though examples of the latter do make use of the term "universe as a whole" in the course of setting out their individual claims, does not by itself guarantee that there does exist an entity for which the expression "the universe as a whole" is a successfully referring name. I conclude, then, thus far, that if we wish to regard the use of the expression "the universe as a whole" as a name for a putative entity, its meaning could not be explained by the ordinarily successful technique of using examples.

Most cosmological models employing the concept of the universe as a whole (or as some prefer to say, simply, "the universe") are grounded on a widely shared world picture so much taken for granted that it may hardly be noticed. It is a world picture permeated by two groups of concepts of special interest to our present study. One is associated with a "creational" picture of the world, illustrated by Plato's *Timaeus*, with the latter's ideas variously incorporated in Judaic, Christian, and Muslim theologies. The other is some version of an "Augustinian picture" of language, with the latter's stress on a word-object, name-entity approach to the nature of meaning. The notion of the universe as a whole found in most cosmological models and traditional philosophies of science is embedded in a world picture with the foregoing historical roots and sources of influence. When, for example, Einstein thinks of the universe as a whole as that whose structure he sets out to articulate in his cosmological model, there can be no doubt he speaks for many who share his own traditional realist preconceptions in this regard. In his "Autobiographical Notes," for example, Einstein makes it clear that for him "Physics is an attempt conceptually to grasp reality as it is thought independently of its being observed. In this sense one speaks of 'physical reality.' "[22] In the context of this world picture and its associated concept of physical reality, the use of the concept of "the universe as a whole" by most cosmologists is taken as a name, a referring device for an independently existing, already determinately structured, intelligible entity. To question this interpretation of the expression "the universe as a whole" is to challenge something so fundamental it would be strongly resisted. Indeed, its hold on our thought and speech is so unrelenting that even to someone ready to question, loosen, or abandon its grip, it will frequently return, willy-nilly, in the course of conveying his own thoughts. Nevertheless, it can be questioned and replaced—at the cost, however, we must concede, of modifying certain aspects of the commonly shared world picture.

Let us assume that from among various competing cosmological models, one model is widely accepted at a particular stage of inquiry by the community of cosmologists. Let us use the expression "the known universe" to designate this preferred account. Since there have been various candidates for "the known universe"—as the history of cosmology surely establishes—and if we expect that for as long as cosmological inquiry will continue into the indefinite future, there will be a succession of candidates for this description, can we nevertheless contrast all of these with an independently real, trans-human, yet unknown reality that we may denominate *the Universe*, of which all "known universes" whether past, present, or in the indefinite future are only "masks"? Some have argued for the merit, indeed the inescapability of this idea, even though one cannot give a full account

[22] P. A. Schilpp, ed., *Albert Einstein: Philosopher-Scientist*, vol. VII (Evanston, Ill.: The Library of Living Philosophers, 1949), 80.

now of what it is, nor will one ever be able to do so. As one sponsor of this thesis affirms:

> Intuitively, the Universe is the unknown (or incompletely known) whole about whose parts physics attempts (or ought to attempt) to give us descriptions and explanations that are true and complete. There is not much one can do to make this intuitive idea more specific. Even though the whole it speaks of is a spatiotemporal whole, no one yet knows which spacetime is involved, or even whether it is any of the space-times that so far have occurred to us. Hence we do not know specifically what we mean when we speak of the whole that is the Universe, or of its parts, which physics attempts to describe and explain, since the definition of a whole requires that a spacetime be specified. [W]e can ill afford to charac-terize the Universe by reference to what physics might some-day achieve, even should physics be practiced ideally and forever.[23]

If, by the author's own admission "we do not know specifically what we mean when we speak of the the whole that is the Uni-verse," it would seem not only futile but nonsensical to continue to affirm the existence or reality of the Universe. The continued adherence to this belief in the reality of a "true physical Uni-verse" beyond the "manifest [known] universe as conceived by today's physics,"[24] even though called an "intuitive" commit-ment, would seem to be wholly gratuitous. It is the last vestige, the still weakly clinging affirmation and faint echo of a Platonic world picture. It can be relinquished without any loss by any phi-losophy that seeks to understand the operative procedures and cri-teria of evaluation of scientific cosmology.

Let us assume that the foregoing considerations concerning the use of the expression "the universe as a whole" as a means for

---

[23] John F. Post, *The Faces of Existence* (Ithaca, N.Y., and London: Cornell University Press, 1987), 156–157.
[24] Post, *Faces of Existence*, 158.

designating an obviously given or even putatively existing object or entity have a sufficiently damaging quality to weaken, if not totally destroy and eliminate, the attraction of using this expression in this way. If there does not exist an entity named by the phrase "the universe as a whole," then the correlated presuppositions that (1) such an entity has certain properties, (2) that it is the task of a cosmological model to discover and set out what these are, and (3) that such a proper disclosure would constitute the truth of a cosmological model, all go by the board. This does not mean that we could not continue to use the notion of truth in connection with cosmological models, provided we redefine in what its truth would consist. And we should still face two possibilities. One is to drop the use of the phrase "the universe as a whole" altogether in describing the goals of a cosmological model. The other is to retain the use of the phrase, though not as designating an existing object or entity. In the latter case, it will be necessary to make clear what its new role will be and to explain its meaning along wholly different lines from those relied on by those consciously or unconsciously influenced by the creational world picture.

These different lines were already pursued, in one form, by Kant in his *Critique of Pure Reason*, where, in the course of rejecting the specious cosmological speculations described in the "Transcendental Dialectic," he undertook to reinterpret what would be a legitimate and fruiful way of pursuing cosmological inquiry.[25] In applying the insights contained in Wittgenstein's critique of language to the field of cosmology, a principal project of my own present inquiry is to show how to explain the role of the expression "the universe as a whole" in ways that are in the spirit, if not the details, of Kant's own views. Our next task is to see how we might give such an account and apply it to making sense of what is accomplished in the pursuit of cosmology.

As our earlier discussion has suggested, the principal functions of a cosmological model may be best summarized as falling into three main groups: (1) innovative *descriptive interpretation* of observed facts; (2) *finding solutions* in the form of physical, causal explanations for problems posed by certain observational data; and (3) *prediction* of fresh observational objects, occurrences, or regularities. When seen in relation to the observable universe as already known, these functions perform the role of *extending the range*, wherever possible, both in terms of observability and understanding, of the scope and limits of the observable universe.

Normally, all three of the above-mentioned roles are intertwined and performed by a particular model through its leading idea. The worth of the leading idea will accordingly be judged in terms of how well it performs all three of these functions. Nevertheless, while there are important interconnections among the three roles—hence also in the use of the term "truth" as a collective term of appraisal for their joint accomplishments—there are also important differences in the kinds of criteria and grounds for using the term "truth" in relation to each of the discriminated functions.

Consider, as an example, the principal conceptual innovation introduced by Einstein in his original cosmological model of 1917. As contrasted with a reliance on the use of traditional concepts of gravitation and space to describe a rich fund of observational data both terrestrial and astronomical, the leading idea of Einstein's earliest cosmological model made use of new ways of conceiving of the nature of gravitation and space. When Einstein undertook to apply these redefined concepts for purposes of giving an account of the uniform spatial distribution of the "stars" (later specified in terms of galaxies), when considered on a cosmic scale, his new description of this material made use of the chief ideas of the general theory of relativity. According to that theory, a gravitational field is to be interpreted not as due to the presence of a *force* exerted by one or more bodies on another, but as arising from the presence of a purely geometric property of *curvature*. As compared to the older, classic Newtonian approach, which treated gravitation as a force exerted mutually by bodies upon one another—a force that Newton himself acknowledged he could not explain (he said *"hypotheses non fingo"*)—Einstein's conception of gravitation and space was based on a geometric interpretation that took advantage of relatively recent advances in non-Euclidean and differential geometry. It was this basic reorientation in thinking of gravitation as a special property *of space* that Einstein used as the key to describing the spatial structure of the universe as a whole. This reinterpretation possessed the merits of elegance, simplicity, and genuine plausibility, along with other advantages. Nevertheless, this was not tantamount to having the ability to give direct observational confirmation for the idea. It could not show by direct observational inspection that that's the way the universe is "in fact"—at least not in the same sense in which, for example, by the use of a theory one is able observationally to discover and locate a hitherto unobserved planet or other object. The redescription remained just that, a matter of applying a new mode of representation, a new grammar or conceptual scheme—or as some might prefer to say, a new "theory"—for interpreting observational data. The new description is not shown to be *true* by comparison with "the facts." For the choice and status of the new conceptual scheme, as of any grammar (whether new or old) is autonomous, a matter of human decision. There are no independent facts already existing in nature to which our grammar has to accommodate itself by matching those putative facts. For to *say what* the "facts" are already presupposes the use of some grammar; these "facts" cannot be guaranteed to inhere in the world apart from the use of a grammar. The criteria for choosing the Einsteinian way of giving sense to the concepts "gravitation" and "space," in preference to other grammars using perhaps the same linguistic expressions, is a pragmatic matter, of the degree to which one finds the revised descriptions of observational data superior to conventional ways of describing them.

Another major role performed by a cosmological model is to offer proposals for solving recognized problems with respect to certain observational data. It does so by suggesting causal mechanisms that would help explain certain acknowledged features of those materials and thereby to remove the problems posed by them. A clear example of this role is the way in which the inflationary model explains the observed isotropy of the cosmic background 3°K radiation, and the virtually similar quantitative values of the actual density of matter and the critical density— features that pose what are called, respectively, the horizon and flatness problems. In judging the truth of the inflationary model, or for that matter any other model insofar as it is also considered with respect to its ability to solve particular problems, the criteria employed are obviously of a different character from those employed in evaluating the truth of a model with respect to its capacities for giving a satisfactory innovative redescription of certain observational materials. For on the level of problem solving, the primary question is this: Does the proposed solution (e.g., that given by the inflationary model, in introducing the notion of an exponentially increasing expansion of space) actually *solve* the problems? The explanation may rely, as it does in the case of the inflationary model, on a physical mechanism already well recognized and previously worked out in standard thermodynamic theory. In applying these standard ideas to the special problem areas, the question is whether they work. A further point worth noting about the problem-solving role of cosmological models is that the problems may relate only to certain selected aspects of the observable universe. Indeed, in the case of the inflationary model (having dealt with the flatness and horizon problems by clarifying the physical mechanisms involved in the very short time period within the first second after the Big Bang), it largely left unchanged all other descriptions and explanations of the evolutionary stages of development of the universe both before this period and for the long stretch afterward. After giving its own description and explanation of how the phase transition was completed, the inflationary model merges its own account with that given in the standard Hot Big Bang model of the evolutionary development of the universe.

A third major role of a cosmological model is to offer predic-

186

tions of novel, observationally identifiable occurrences and objects beyond the range and of already identified contents of the known observable universe. This predictive role offers another direction and level in which the truth of a cosmological model is judged. Here again, the criteria for making appraisals of truth or falsity have a special focus. They do not concern the "aptness" or "illuminating quality" of an interpretative redescription of already obtained observational data, nor the workability of suggested physical explanations for problem areas. They concern, instead, the question whether the existence of certain objects and occurrences beyond the range of the already known observable region are in fact observed and can be interpreted with the aid of the distinctive conceptual tools of the model under consideration. This calls, in the first place, for observational confirmation or disconfirmation of predictions; success is measured by the amount, accuracy, and repeatability of such confirmations. It also involves, in the second place, the advantages of interpreting the newly confirmed observational data with the aid of the concepts of the theory that led to their discovery. If successful on this level, a cosmological model adds to the storehouse of both information and understanding. It helps to *enlarge* the scope of the known and understood observable universe.

Insofar as cosmology can be reckoned among the empirical sciences, it must apply and test its conceptual claims by resorting to available observational data. In the end, any cosmological model will need to pay its respects to all the relevant observational materials—although, as previously noted, not all such materials occupy the same level or degree of reliability and accuracy. Moreover, different cosmological models pay differential regard to the fund of available observational data: the leading idea of a particular cosmological model may pay special attention to only selected parts of this fund. Thus the observational data given special prominence in the early stages of the development of relativistic cosmology had to do with the uniform (isotropic, homogeneous), large-scale, spatial distribution of the galaxies and with the Hubble law concerning their redshifts. Similarly, the application of recent theories of particle physics in understanding the early, very early, and even pre-Big Bang stages of the development of the universe, have dealt with such observational data as the isotropy of the $3°K$ microwave background radiation, the relative abundances of the elements, the closeness of the actual density to the critical density of matter-energy in the universe, the predominance of matter over antimatter, the high photon-baryon ratio, the differentiation among the four fundamental forces at the present stage of the universe, the clumpiness of matter in the form of individual galaxies, galactic clusters, and superclusters, and so on. Not all proposed cosmological models give active consideration to all of these observational data or deal with them in the same way. On the side, too, of interpretation, models differ among themselves in the conceptual tools brought to bear. Sometimes, as in the case of models of relativistic cosmology, there is emphasis on the geometric approach to understanding gravitation. However, the presence of gravitation on the subatomic level is approached by recent quantum field theories, quantum gravity theories, and supersymmetry and superstring theories in ways that are considerably different from the original "geometric curvature of a field" view of Einstein's general theory of relativity. In short, different cosmological models offer a varied battery of conceptual tools for explaining, classifying, and rendering intelligible the data of observation.

A summary judgment of the degree of "total truth" of a cosmological model is arrived at by taking into account the adequacy and success with which it performs all three of the roles of redescription, explanation, and prediction, and as judged, too, on these levels, by comparison with the relative merits of available competing models. It is by summing over, assigning "weights," and taking into account the particular degree of success (truth) on each level that one reaches an appraisal of the comparative total degree of truth of a model. Once again, this result tells us something about the merits of a conceptual scheme when applied for these diverse purposes, not about whether there is a set of facts "in the universe" that independently possesses its own structure and properties that the conceptual scheme discloses. This conception of truth is a pragmatic one, not one of correspondence with antecedent fact. It locates the appraisal of truth within the process of a continuing, historically located inquiry, and not in the context of some putatively fixed, inquiry-independent ontological state of affairs.

The goal of cosmology, thus envisaged, is one of *enlargement* of the range of cosmological knowledge beyond the limits of the observable universe as known at a particular stage of inquiry. This search for enlargement of knowledge is tantamount to a search for ways of observationally and intellectually locating the observable universe, as identified at a particular stage of inquiry, within *a more inclusive domain*. This larger domain may even be designated as "the universe as a whole," if this is understood as the maximally largest physical system that can be understood with theoretic resources available at a given stage of inquiry. However, this "maximally intelligible physical system" changes content with advances in theory, and is not fixed conceptually in the history of inquiry. In a sense, therefore, the pursuit of cosmological inquiry, insofar as it is taken to be concerned with "the universe as a whole," is never completed, since the same goal stated in these general terms will always be appropriate, no matter how far inquiry has continued or how much "larger" the scope of observation or understanding will have been reached. Once we surrender the presupposition that the phrase "the universe as a whole" designates an entity existing independently of inquiry, possessed of its own intrinsic properties, and awaiting disclosure in an account that will be appraised as true to the extent that the account matches the actual state of affairs in the entity being investigated, we may retain the expression "the universe as a whole," provided we recognize that it performs a different role from the one associated with the familiar, realistic Platonic usage. One might still use the phrase "the universe as a whole" to refer to the subject matter for cosmology, provided this phrase is used simply as a shorthand way of encompassing the aforementioned three principal roles and goals of cosmology. When so understood, the expression "the universe as a whole" is not a name for an object or entity, observable or unobservable. It is a way of referring to the descriptive, explanatory, and predictive powers of a cosmological model when these powers are exercised with respect to the observable data already obtained or awaiting confirmation. Such data have to do with existent objects, events, and processes that belong to the observable universe.

In the foregoing, my principal effort has been to demythologize the strong hold of the notion of the universe as a whole as this is commonly understood, and the belief in the unquestionable existence of an object or entity to which this term supposedly refers. I have urged that the actual role of cosmological inquiry is to engage in the unending task of enlarging the scope of knowledge with respect to the observable universe. This is to be done through enlarging the range and detail of identification of its contents and by achieving an understanding of those contents. If accepted, this interpretation has the broad consequence of regarding what we mean by "the universe," and the truth of a model that purports to set out its nature, as being open to continual revision and therefore as not controlled or determined by the independent existence and inherent structure of some all-inclusive entity. This means that we should recognize a certain inescapable epistemological and ontological indefiniteness and incompletability in the subject matter of cosmology. There is nothing incoherent in such a view, although it is, admittedly—for those firmly entrenched in opposite and traditional ways of thought— undoubtedly such.

To the question, then, "Does the universe as a whole exist?" my answer is "Yes, provided you accept my own earlier account, with its redefinitions of 'the universe as a whole' and 'truth.' If you do, what will have been accomplished is to have shifted attention from the matter of settling the question of the existence of an all-inclusive object or entity, called 'the universe,' 'the universe as a whole,' or 'the Universe' into having an altered conception of *truth* as it concerns a *cosmological model*." The primary interest in the construction and testing of cosmological models belongs to an indefinitely prolonged course of inquiry. I say "indefinitely prolonged" not as a matter that leaves open the question of how far into the future the pursuit of cosmology by human beings will continue, but rather, no matter how long it does continue, that has to do with the character of that pursuit. For in that pursuit there will always be the possibility of new conceptual schemes, new grammars, and new leading ideas in the fashioning of cosmological models. Their construction by human beings is an autonomous affair, not beholden to the disclosure of or success in matching the structure of an independently existing entity. The goal and step-by-step achievements in the pursuit of cosmology are measured, instead, by the success achieved in enlarging the scope of human knowledge of the observable universe.

SIX

Boundless Existence

In the previous chapter we explored the scope of cosmology as a scientific discipline by approaching it in terms of the distinction between the observable universe and the universe as a whole, and by considering how this distinction bears on answering the question "Does the universe exist?" If we accept the general results reached, we face the further question whether this would suffice, along with appropriate elaboration of details, for an adequate reply to the question of reality. Does the existence of the observable universe, and what can be established as its contents and structure, exhaust all that belongs to Reality in its most fundamental nature? If not, what more needs to be said? The answer I wish to propose is that there *is* something more.

I will use the expression "Boundless Existence" to designate this "something more." I will use it to refer to a crucial aspect of Reality beyond or transcendent to that of the observable universe insofar as the latter is understood. This transcendent aspect of Reality, however, should not be equated with the fact that the observable universe, for scientific cosmology, is unendingly open to further enlargement both on the levels of increasing information (through enrichment of the fund of observational data) and through bringing to bear novel forms of conceptual understanding. Boundless Existence always outstrips and transcends any actual or possible scientific knowledge of the known universe.

Boundless Existence always looms as the "unintelligible more," no matter how far scientific understanding has progressed. As the transcendent aspect of Reality, Boundless Existence is not accessible either to observation or to scientific understanding by human beings, hence not open to investigation by either means. A scientific enlargement of knowledge of the observable universe leaves untouched and undiminished the transcendent unintelligibility of Boundless Existence.

But this does not mean that we could obtain reliable knowledge of Boundless Existence by metaphysical means. For there are no properties or structural features belonging to Boundless Existence that are open to discovery and conceptual articulation by metaphysics, any more than it is the case they could be investigated by science. The term "Boundless Existence," accordingly, will hereinafter be used to refer to an aspect of Reality that totally frustrates any search for intelligibility, whether this search is carried out by science *or* metaphysics.

What the term "Boundless Existence" stands for is best approached by pursuing a number of different routes, all of which, if successfully followed, converge on the same result. That result is always "there"—open to a type of intensified *awareness*, though not to any form of *understanding or knowledge*. The awareness, consequently, is an experience wholly different from that in which it is possible to discriminate various properties or a structural pattern in some subject matter and which, when found, can be described in language.

The awareness of Boundless Existence represents the focal point in a world picture that undertakes to challenge the historically dominant Platonic emphasis on cosmic and metaphysical intelligibility. A principal goal of the present investigation, in its inclusion of Boundless Existence alongside the observable universe as a principal feature of the world picture it proposes, is to show the consequences that flow from surrendering the pervasive guidance of the model of "rational art" in metaphysics. In pursuing this goal, I do not dwell on the differences (important as they are) between Plato's conception of the Demiurge and the theist's conception of God. For both philosophies share adherence to the use of the central concept of cosmic creation and its image of a guiding supernatural intelligence. The use of this concept and image satisfies a human craving to find omnipresent intelligible order in the world at large. In opposition to this familiar approach, the metaphysics that gives a central place to the notion of Boundless Existence entails abandoning the concept of cosmic creation, together with the associated idea of a creative intelligence at work on a superhuman, cosmic level. This rival metaphysical view springs from rejecting the all-too-ready propensity of human beings (frequently carried to fanatical and dogmatic extremes) to think that what we, as human beings, would like to be the case—that there must be a reason for everything—is to be satisfied by believing in the existence of a transcendent creative intelligence whose activity is evidenced by the intelligible character of the world it creates. Out of this propensity and eagerness to project our human desires for rationality and intelligibility onto the world at large are born those world views that rely on the model of "rational art" and its application in the form of the concept of cosmic creation.

One of the consequences of abandoning this model and replacing it with an awareness of the status of Boundless Existence as a fundamental feature of Reality is to offer a radical challenge to the traditional and prevalent acceptance of realist epistemology. According to the latter, there is already embodied in reality a fixed, unique, intelligible order awaiting disclosure and expression in human language. In contrast to such a philosophy, the finding of intelligibility in natural phenomena is seen to be a matter of bringing to bear humanly constructed grammars and using them to convey and articulate ways of *introducing* or creating intelligibility—but not as tools for *uncovering* or discovering intelligibility as an inherent ("in itself") property of the world that exists independently of and antecedently to all human activity of using languages. Rather than look for the embodiment in the world of conceptual planning by a superhuman intelligence as the grounds for finding intelligibility in the world, we should restrict the activity of finding intelligibility to the use of humanly created linguistic means.

On the view here proposed, the drive by reason, as traditionally pursued, to discover order and intelligibility *in* the world is blocked—not because of human limitations and incompetence, but because there is a fundamental, inherent aspect of *unintelligibility* both in the very existence of the world and in what it is "in itself" apart from the use of humanly devised conceptual schemes. It is the radical presence on a metaphysical level of this aspect of unintelligibility—defeating all actual or possible efforts by human reason to *discover* intelligible order everywhere—that is brought to the fore in recognizing Boundless Existence as a crucial aspect of Reality.

In general, then, the proper locus and application of the concept of rational art and associated efforts at establishing examples of intelligible order are found *within* the domain of human experience and human life, where, through human creative efforts, its instances are realized in varying degrees and forms. I must stress, accordingly, that in proposing this radical shift in the search for intelligible order, the world view I propose here does *not* involve undervaluing the role of rationality and intelligibility or abandoning the human efforts toward their realization. It involves, rather, recognizing the limits to the human search for such intelligibility on a metaphysical level. As contrasted with traditional conceptions, it reassigns the locus and source of finding intelligibility in Reality.

In the foregoing, I have used the expression "unintelligibility" to describe, on a metaphysical level, the nature of Reality, and have proposed to use the expression "Boundless Existence" as a device for focusing on and representing this feature of Reality. To avoid misinterpretation, and in any case to explore somewhat more fully what is bound up with ascribing unintelligibility to Reality, we must disentangle and make clear a number of related themes and draw some necessary distinctions. Two main questions call for examination. If, contrary to those who adopt a realist epistemology in describing the goals and achievements of science, we say that *there is no unique intelligible order already present "in itself" in the world* awaiting discovery, what does such unintelligibility amount to? We shall find that in answering this question, we are led to one aspect of Boundless Existence. And if, contrary to the theist, we say that the *existence* of the world is unintelligible, what does this mean? To answer this question, I will propose that Boundless Existence is another crucial mark of such unintelligibility and applies to the known observable universe, whatever the extent of any scientific knowledge of the latter.

A characteristic and recurrent feature of many metaphysical world views is the effort to identify a "primary" type of reality. Everything else recognized by the metaphysics to possess its own distinctive mode of actual or possible existence will then be assigned some form of derivative or ancillary status with respect to the primary reality. With the primary reality taken as foundation, source, or basis for comparison with everything else, descriptions and explanations are offered for the origin, role, rank, and position of all "derivative" entities. Depending on the type of metaphysical view involved, the relation between the primary reality and its derivatives is differently specified—for example, deductively, causally, teleologically, hierarchically, or by exemplification. Thus, Democritus maintained that reality at its most fundamental level consists of "atoms and the void." Plato was convinced of the eternal reality of Intelligible Forms and regarded everything else as being, at best, their derivative approximations and exemplifications. Theists assign absolute metaphysical primacy to God. Spinoza chose Substance (Nature or God) as that in terms of which everything is be understood. For Heidegger, Being (*Sein*) is absolutely fundamental. And so on.

The choice in my own metaphysical investigation of a candidate for "primary reality" is *the observable universe*. According to this approach, the observable universe—identified according to the best available knowledge of scientific cosmology—serves as the preferred starting point for metaphysical inquiry. When applied to the observable universe, the terms "observable," "intelligible," and "exist" are used with due allowances for various qualifications, exceptions, and degrees of tentativeness and controversiality. Thus, rather than think of the term "observable universe" as standing for a single, readily identifiable "object" or "entity," it is better that we draw necessary distinctions among the various component astronomical objects, systems of objects, phenomena, horizons, phenomenologically established laws reporting measured and observed regularities, and applications of physical theories for describing, explaining, and predicting observational data; and so on. In the course of listing and examining the various "contents" and acknowledged "limits" of observability that characterize the observable universe at a particular stage of inquiry, it is obvious that we must be wary of making a wholesale judgment about what belongs to the observable universe or is true of it. Instead, it is important to consider distributively and seriatim the different components of the observable universe and how to render them intelligible, while taking into account the varying degrees of consensus among qualified experts about these matters. Any resulting compound judgment is one, if made, that is not likely to elicit universal agreement about the truth of various details comprising the compound judgment, nor would its detailed content be static and closed when the process of scientific inquiry is viewed historically. In short, what belongs to the observable universe and what can be said to be understood about it are not a uniform matter, easily summed up.

Despite all the foregoing necessary qualifications and cautionary remarks that would discourage using the term "observable universe" for scientific purposes in a simple, wholesale, and naive way, it remains the case that, having made these qualifications, we can still affirm, in behalf of metaphysical purposes of the sort we are here interested in, that there is a reasonably steady, established core of observable results and qualifiedly true judgments arrived at by competent investigators that warrant the truth of the statement, "The observable universe exists and can be made intelligible."

Insofar as we find the need to introduce the notion of Boundless Existence, it is because, in trying to understand the observable universe, we *also* encounter in certain respects the fact of the latter's radical *unintelligibility*. In offering an answer to the question of reality, we are thereby led to the thesis that one must give special prominence not only to the observable universe and the sense in which it is *intelligible*, but also to Boundless Existence and thereby to the sense in which the observable universe is *unintelligible*.

In order to indicate the types of consideration that lead to recognizing Boundless Existence as a fundamental aspect of Reality and to making clear in what sense the observable universe is unintelligible, we need, first of all, to distinguish two principal ways in which the term "exist" can be used in connection with the observable universe. Having done this, we should also recall the distinction we made earlier between the two principal ways (the Platonic and Kantian) in which the term "intelligible" can be used—a distinction that will clarify in what sense we can say Boundless Existence is unintelligible.

I turn, first, to distinguish two principal uses of the term "exist." One is the sense in which we say that various items found in the known observable universe exist, the other is employed in the nominalized and capitalized expression, "Boundless Existence."

The first of these two senses of "existence" comes to the fore wherever, for example, from the perspective of a cosmologist's interest, one asks for the criteria for establishing whether something exists, and—given these criteria and applying them—what confirming evidence there is for accepting a particular account as a true description or explanation of some feature of the observable universe. Where confirming evidence is available that supports the description or explanation being considered, one says of some object, occurrence, process, or regularity that it exists. The use of the term "galaxy" (specified in one or another of its special types) is an accepted description for certain visually or otherwise perceived and measured data. Evidence can be offered in particular cases to support the classification and description as true—as establishing the existence of galaxies. The microwave background radiation is another existent feature of the observable universe. So is the law or regularity reporting the fact that the redshifts of galaxies is linearly correlated with their distance. So is the fact that the value of the cosmological constant (the difference between the critical density of mass and the actual density) is close to zero. And so on. In each case there are normally available conceptual tools for describing these specific features of the observable universe and for accepting these descriptions as true—as reporting existing features or components of the observable universe. In addition, of course, there are further questions that arise concerning how to *explain* these features. Where such explanations are forthcoming, additional considerations come to the fore concerning the criteria to be employed in accepting them as true when applied, and therefore for determining in what sense, or to what extent, the explanation also points to something existent in the observable universe. In this process of rendering some existent feature of the observable universe intelligible, we must recognize, of course, that any achieved successes may involve giving explanations that depend at some point on taking some other matters as unexplained, but not necessarily as unexplainable, by science. We must expect, therefore, that no cognitive enlargement of the observable universe by the use of scientific resources will ever eventuate in the finding of an account in which there are no further questions to be asked or possibly answered. This amounts to accepting the view that there will never be an absolute terminus to the search for scientific intelligibility with respect to existent features or contents of the observable universe, whatever the extent of the cumulative successes of science at any particular stage of inquiry.

Thus far, let us assume, there are no intractable objections to using the ordinary term "exists" in application to the observable universe and its contents. There is, however, another, special use of the term "exists" (or its nominative form "existence") that comes to the fore and that leads to the use of the qualifying term "boundless" in connection with it. Here the term "boundless" will be used, not in any quantitative or metric sense, but rather to signify the total absence, inapplicability, and radical unavailability of *any* form of description or explanation: of the use of any scheme of *conceptual bounds*. The ordinary or scientific use of the term "exists" ("existent," or "existence"), previously alluded to, does not provide any occasion or incentive for using the qualifying adjective "boundless" in this way. We should not come upon Boundless Existence in considering this or that feature of the known observable universe as described, questioned, explained, or understood at any stage of scientific cosmological inquiry.

I shall distinguish two major routes to this latter, special sense of "exists," viz., "Exists" or its nominalization, "Existence." One route to this special sense is best recaptured by stressing the kinds of metaphysical questions raised by traditional theology about the existence of the world. The other route to the special use of "exists" is of a more directly epistemological character.

Let us consider, to begin with, the special use of the term "exists" that arises from taking a primarily metaphysical orientation of the sort to which the theist directs our attention. In a theistic metaphysics, one starts with the fact *that* the observed world exists and that it has a determinable structure and contents. For the sake of brevity, I shall refer to the latter (its structure and contents) as its *what*. By asking "*Why* does the world exist at all?" and "*Why* does it have *what* properties (the structure and contents) it does?" and by answering these questions by relying on the creation model, the resulting main feature of theistic metaphysics (whatever its manifold variations in detail) is based on a fundamental division into two main entities: the created world and its Creator. Each "entity" (the created world, and God as Creator) has its own *that* (its own mode or level of existence) and its own *what* (its own set of properties and attributes). As it concerns both the existence of the world and its properties, the *why* question is given an answer: God created it.

Part of the intellectual price paid in accepting this answer is to admit that while we are assured, whether by argument, analogy, faith, or revelation, *that* God exists, we do not have any detailed knowledge of the *what* of God. Furthermore, it is commonly claimed, it makes no sense to ask the question "Why?" concerning God's existence. Accordingly, while this metaphysical view achieves its own type of consistency and simplification by answering the "why" question concerning the existence and properties of the observed world, an acceptance of this answer also carries with it an *increase* in the number of mysteries and unanswerable questions. These include God's own "that," "why," "what," and "how," as well as those surrounding the lack of full human understanding of God's purposes in establishing various features of the world. The latter type of unanswerability holds for the kinds of questions raised in the *Book of Job*.

It will not serve our present interest to rehearse the familiar history of attempts to prove the existence of God or to examine the equally familiar criticisms and "rebuttals" of these arguments. If we accept Wittgenstein's analysis of how we should regard the beliefs that make up a world picture of whatever sort as distinguished from "fluid" or nonfoundational beliefs, then one cannot refute the position of the theist. All that can be done is to rely on the possible effectiveness of "persuasion" to bring about a change in the groundless commitments that define his world picture.

I shall confine myself, therefore, to examining the point from which the theist's metaphysics takes its departure: the conviction that there *must* be a reason for the very existence of the world, whatever the success of science in explaining the existence of one or another detail or aspect of the observable universe. It is this conviction of "mustness" that fuels and supports all efforts at meeting the metaphysical hunger for an explanation of the existence of the world.

Let us use the capitalized term "Existence" in connection with the observable universe to refer to what is disclosed in the awareness *that* the observable universe exists—whatever the particular features of the observable universe and their actual or possible scientific explanation. In this sense, Existence lies beyond the range of any conceptual tools of the sort that science employs in its dealings with the observable universe. *It is the having of this awareness of the fact that the universe Exists, that our own world picture shares with the viewpoint of the theist.* It serves as the matrix from which our respective, though ultimately divergent metaphysical journeys take their common point of departure.

Given *that* the known observable universe Exists, whatever its observed or scientifically understood features may be at any stage of the enlargement of the known observable universe, those who adopt the viewpoint of the traditional theist ask: Should we not be able to ask various questions about the "that" (about the Existence) of the known observable universe? Should we not be able to ask, for example, *"How* did it come into Existence?" and *"Why* does it Exist?" If we were able to answer these questions, the fact of the Existence of the observable universe would not be a total mystery; it would be conceptually bound, it would be amenable to encompassment by some conceptual scheme, whether literal, metaphorical or analogical.

It is precisely here where the world picture I am proposing deviates from those who subscribe to the foregoing type of outlook. It takes the "that" of the world's Existence, of which we have an awareness, as *not* amenable to any form of conceptual understanding. It leaves the Existence of the observable universe a not further analyzable, describable, or explainable metaphysical fact: a groundless aspect of Reality. It finds no justification for the belief in being able successfully to find reasons for the Existence of the observable universe in any of the various standard uses of the expression "reason."[1]

As approached in the present account, Boundless Existence is not an entity of a special type, as, for example, God is thought to be: one having a mind, creative abilities, solicitude for human beings, causal efficacy, and so on. Boundless Existence is not an entity at all. Instead, in the search for intelligibility and the fulfillment of that search through the use of humanly produced

---

[1] For a discussion, in some detail, see my book, *The Mystery of Existence*, chaps. 10 and 11.

conceptual schemes, we restrict ourselves to distinguishing the "that" and the "what" of the various contents of the observable universe, as well as asking, with the scientist, various types of "why" questions about the details of the observable universe. However, the Existence of the known observable universe remains altogether outside the scope and powers of conferring intelligibility upon it by means of a standard conceptual sort. An acknowledgment of this unintelligibility is one aspect of what is signified by the use of the term "Boundless Existence." Boundless Existence is a way of referring to the total unintelligibility of the Existence of the universe, regardless of how much intelligibility science achieves with respect to the existent parts (objects, occurrences, processes, spatial and temporal scope) of the observable universe.

Thus, in the face of the acknowledged fact of the persistent human search for rationality and intelligibility on a metaphysical level, we should pose our own form of "why" question: Why need the very Existence of the world (apart from the existence of its internal details and observable features) be explainable? Mystery for mystery, why should we not allow that the Existence of the world is beyond all possible explanation? Why should we not regard the very Existence of the observable universe as a metaphysical datum in the same way as God's existence is accepted by the theist as that which must remain forever unintelligible? And why should we not ascribe the unintelligibility of the Existence of the observable universe, not to the fact of our human "finitude" and incapacity to find such a reason, but simply to the fact that the world's Existence is that for which the search for a reason is unsatisfiable? An awareness of Boundless Existence would then consist in the realization that the Existence of the observable universe is unintelligible: an irreducible and ineliminable feature of Reality. "Boundless Existence" could then serve as a way of emphasizing the metaphysical fact that inevitable failure faces any search to find an answer to the question "Why is there a universe at all?" In this respect, and to the extent we equate the "question of reality" with a search for an answer to the question "Why does the universe Exist at all?" there is *no answer*.

So much for a brief review of the basically different ways of responding to the awareness of the Existence of the universe—that of the theist and of our own account—and why, according to the latter, this awareness is accompanied by the realization that Existence is unintelligible: that it is conceptually Boundless.

In addition to the foregoing way of approaching the notion of Boundless Existence as signifying the unintelligibility (the unavailability of an explanation) of the Existence of the observable universe—and thus in opposition to the Platonic view that there is such an explanation and that the "question of reality" *can be answered*—there is another route that leads to the same conclusion. This is the route of epistemology. It does not fasten, as does the first route we have just briefly explored, on attempts to solve the mystery of Existence—to answering the question "*Why* does the universe Exist at all?" Instead, it focuses primarily on the question of the *what* of the observable universe: its having a certain structure and contents. And it seeks to answer the following kinds of questions: In what does the intelligibility of the contents and structure of the universe consist? In what sense, or to what extent, can we as human beings hope to understand and know the nature of that intelligible order? What is the source of this intelligibility? On what grounds do claims to have been able to establish intelligibility rest? And if sustained, what makes any such claims true? These questions are of a fundamentally epistemological sort.

The variety of ways in which these questions have been answered again points to a fundamental divergence in philosophical viewpoints. The divergence centers on the different ways of interpreting the meaning of "intelligibility": the Platonic and Kantian ways. As we have seen, the Kantian way, which we have followed here, offers its own way of analyzing what is involved in saying that the observable universe *can* be made intelligible. If by the "question of reality" one means "How can we describe and explain (render intelligible) the various observable features (the 'what') of the observable universe?" then, for the Kantian, *this* question can be answered. It consists in the application of humanly created sets of "grammatical rules," as in science, to the materials of observational experience, and by making the choice from among available proposals of those that prove most successful in practice. This process of creating conceptual schemes for purposes of description and explanation, and of choosing at a particular stage of inquiry the most successful ones, is an unending one when considered historically. The evaluation of "success" is not determined by looking among competing accounts for that one which matches perfectly (or even with increasing approximation and probability) the supposedly unique, objective, independently existing structure of the world "in itself." The "question of reality," if interpreted as asking for the criteria to be used in describing and explaining the materials of observational experience, is *not to be answered in a Platonic way*, that is, by finding which is the inherent, unique, intelligible order already implanted in the world by a Divine Intelligence. It involves, rather, a comparison of any proposed conceptual scheme with rival accounts that are also products of human creative intelligence. The goal is to see which, among available schemes, is *better* than any of the others available at a given stage of inquiry. There need be no presumption that there is a *best* one, and that it will be found when human beings will be able to match the unique pattern of intelligibility already supposedly embedded in the world in itself. If we surrender all reliance on and appeal to the analogy of craftsmanship on a cosmic and metaphysical level, as in the Platonic model, then the idea that the world contains "in itself" some discoverable, unique intelligible structure goes with it. This conception of the "in itself" is the echo and relic of the craftsman model and should be abandoned.

If, despite the foregoing objections against using the Platonic sense of an intelligible order in the world "in itself," we wish nevertheless to retain, from a Kantian perspective, the use of the expression "in itself," this can be done only by saying that what is "in itself" is the Existence of the observable universe. Man does not create the Existence of the observable universe. Human beings, at most, are *aware that* the observable universe Exists. But *what* the Existence of the observable universe is "in itself" is unintelligible. The Existence of the observable universe "in itself" gives no foothold for the application of descriptive expressions or explanatory theories, no basis for exemplifying the use of general terms in predicative position.

In this respect, the "that" of the Existence of the observable universe is to be contrasted with the "that" of a recognized existent part or phase of development *within* the observable universe. *That* this person, or this building, this blade of grass, this thunderstorm, this supernova explosion, this planet, exists is open to description and explanation, to the application of some conceptual scheme. Where successful and accepted, the "that" of an existent within the observable universe is thereby made intelligible by links of one sort or another (causal, purposive, historical, etc.) to other existents that are also within the observable universe. But this way of rendering intelligible the "that" of an existent within the observable universe is not available for describing or explaining the "that" of the Existence of the observable universe. The "that" of the Existence of the observable universe has no properties, qualities, or structure of its own. It cannot be described or explained by linkage, via an acceptable scheme, to one or more existents. The Existence of the observable universe is devoid of anything that could sanction this way of thinking. *That* the observable universe Exists is Boundless; it is not "in itself" intelligible. The term "Boundless Existence" is used to mark this unintelligibility.

SUMMARY AND CONCLUSIONS

To sum up our main conclusions: The "positive" answer to the question of reality depends on making and applying appropriate distinctions in the uses of the expressions "existence" and "intelligibility."

In connection with "existence," the basic distinction is between (1) existents within the observable universe, or the observable universe insofar as it is a limited collection of existent objects, events, and processes, and is identified and understood at a particular stage of scientific inquiry; and (2) the Boundless Existence of the observable universe.

In connection with "intelligibility," the basic distinction is between a Platonic and Kantian sense of this term. The observable universe, as known at a given stage of scientific inquiry, *is* intelligible—but only in a Kantian way, not in a Platonic one. However, Boundless Existence, as manifested by the Existence of the observable universe, is unintelligible; it *cannot be rendered intelligible* either in a Platonic way (whether it be through a theistic metaphysics or a philosophy of epistemological realism) or in a Kantian way. It cannot be described or explained by any acceptable conceptual scheme; it is conceptually Boundless. Insofar as the question of reality seeks an answer to *what* the intelligible structure of the Existence of the observable universe is *in itself*, there is *no answer*. Because Reality includes Boundless Existence, and the latter is the locus of a radical unintelligibility "in" Reality, we must also accept the negative conclusion that there is no answer to the question of reality. From this perspective, one must abandon the pursuit of metaphysics as a knowledge-yielding discipline.

The observable universe and Boundless Existence are the two basic aspects or dimensions of Reality—but they are not differentiated from one another by being two distinct types of entities. Boundless Existence is not transcendent to and distinct from the observable universe in the same way in which, according to traditional theology, God is distinct from and transcendent to the world. The presence in Reality of both the observable universe and Boundless Existence is altogether unique. No model or analogy drawn from ordinary experience of what is found in the observable universe will adequately serve to describe the presence in Reality of the observable universe and Boundless Existence.

A final word may be in order as we survey the road we have traveled and the results we have reached. In dealing with "the question of reality" and in indicating to what extent we could say that there is an "answer," and the extent to which there is "no answer," shall we say that the combination of these results (having to do with the respect in which we can predicate intelligibility or unintelligibility of the observable universe or Boundless Existence) constitutes a claim to the *truth* about Reality, and therefore a contribution to *metaphysical knowledge?*

I should reply by taking advantage of Wittgenstein's remarks about the nature of world pictures. What I have offered and suggested is a world picture. The distinctions and "principles" I have worked out are *groundless,* yet for that very reason are basic to the world picture presented. If one stays within this picture, then one might be tempted to claim they offer a type of "knowledge" and can claim "truth." But to say this is to say very little. For the knowledge and truth are of a wholly different sort from the way these terms can be used in connection with the activities and results of a scientific sort. In "doing" metaphysics and emerging with a world picture, there is no appeal to observation and no construction of a theory that can be tested by confrontation with observational materials. Moreover, since the distinctions made and the analyses given of terms such as "knowledge" and "truth" are *internal* to a particular philosophical viewpoint, and since each metaphysical and epistemological view offers its own distinctive rules for explaining these expressions, there is no neutral, independent, external source to which one can appeal to decide which is "really" the case. In short, one cannot give either criteria or evidence of a universally acknowledged sort to uphold the groundless principles selected and appealed to by a particular world picture. All one can do, at best, is to try to persuade others having different principles of the soundness of one's own choices. The world picture I have proposed on a metaphysical level is, in this respect, not different from any other world picture. I can only hope to have made a plausible case for the choices I have made: for the distinctions, analyses, and arguments I have offered.

Index

Index

Index

meaning, of linguistic expressions (Wittgenstein), 81–92, 128

metaphysics, vii–viii, 7–19, 138–139, 193; attempts to eliminate, 10–12, 67ff.; differences and controversies, 9f.; of experience (Kant), 69; metaphysical knowledge, 68–70, 115–119, 193–208; and theology, 49; transcendent variety criticized by Kant, 69; Wittgensteinian critique, 96f.

Milne, E. A., 160–61

models, cosmological, ix, 154–191

Moore, G. E., 106

mystery of existence, 126, 201–204

myths, cosmogonic, 23–25; Plato's *Timaeus*, 31ff., 41–44

names, 82–85

necessity, and knowledge, 70ff., 80f., 98–106

Newton, Isaac, 185

Nietzsche, Friedrich, 5–7

nothing (concept of), 51–64; Aquinas, 56–57; and Boundless Existence, 58, 64; Erigena, 61–63; Kabbalah, 59ff.

noumena (things-in-themselves), 65, 67, 71ff., 105–106, 129

observable universe, x, 144–154, 196–197; enlargement of, 187–191; existence of, 148–154; intelligibility, 149–154, 197; limits and horizons, 146–148

ontology, 7f., 27ff.

origin of the world (myths), 23–25

pantheism, 55

particle physics, viii

Penzias, Arno, 147, 171

Philo Judaeus (fl. 20 B.C.–A.D. 40), 28, 50

philosophy, 3, 9, 80, 95–97; analytic, 97f.; of life, 4f.

Plato, *Timaeus*, 25–49, 180; influence on philosophy of science, 45–48; Intelligible Forms as abstract objects, 84, as primary reality, 196; myth of cosmic creation compared with traditional theism, 49–54; and neo-Platonic emanationism, 54f.; Wittgenstein's criticism of, 87, 115

Plotinus (205–270), 28, 54ff., 57

Post, John F., 182

Proclus (c. 410–485), 47

quantum: reality, 12f.; theories, 167

rational art, 28–30, 129f., 193, 195

realism, 17f., 26–28, 48, 116, 126f., 194; and Boundless Existence, 194ff.; Kant's views, 70ff., 78

reality, vii–x, 7–10, 16, 25, 27, 64, 105f., 123–134; and Boundless Existence, 192–206; conformity to thought (Kant), 71; contrast with appearance, 66f., 105; formulating the question of, 130–134; grammar and reality (Wittgenstein), 89–92, 96f., 101f., 103, 105, 112–113, 128–130; and intelligibility, 123–130; Plato, 25–26; primary reality, 196; and realism, 18, 26–28, 71ff., 126f.; use of term "Reality," 130–131, 133–134; and world pictures, 113–119

reason, 123–125; Kantian, 127–130; Plato, Platonic, 28–30, 125–127

Robertson, H. P., 157

Russell, Bertrand, 137

Ryle, Martin, 172

Saadia (882–942), 56

Scholem, Gershom, 59n, 60, 61

Sciama, Dennis W., 139–143

science, ix, 11–13, 42–46, 66–69,